United States Government Accountability Office

Report to Congressional Requesters

I0448306

September 2013

GREAT LAKES RESTORATION INITIATIVE

Further Actions Would Result in More Useful Assessments and Help Address Factors That Limit Progress

GAO-13-797

September 2013

GREAT LAKES RESTORATION INITIATIVE

Further Actions Would Result in More Useful Assessments and Help Address Factors That Limit Progress

GAO Highlights

Highlights of GAO-13-797, a report to congressional requesters

Why GAO Did This Study

The Great Lakes contain about 84 percent of North America's surface freshwater and provide economic and recreational benefits in the Great Lakes Basin. However, the Great Lakes face significant stresses—such as toxic pollution—that have caused ecological and economic damage to the region.

Approximately $1.3 billion has been appropriated to the GLRI, created in fiscal year 2010, which an interagency Task Force of 11 federal agencies, chaired by the EPA Administrator, oversees. In 2010, the Task Force issued an Action Plan for fiscal years 2010 to 2014 to develop a comprehensive approach to restoring the health of the Great Lakes ecosystem. GAO was asked to review the GLRI. This report examines (1) how the GLRI is implemented by the Task Force agencies and other stakeholders, (2) the methods that EPA has in place to assess GLRI progress, (3) the progress identified by the Task Force agencies and nonfederal stakeholders, and (4) the views of nonfederal stakeholders on factors, if any, that may affect or limit GLRI progress. GAO analyzed the Action Plan, surveyed 205 non-federal recipients of GLRI funding, and interviewed Task Force agency officials and nonfederal stakeholders.

What GAO Recommends

GAO recommends that EPA help ensure more comprehensive and useful GLRI progress assessments and account for factors outside of the Action Plan's scope that may affect the GLRI's long-term success. EPA generally agreed with GAO's recommendations.

View GAO-13-797. For more information, contact J. Alfredo Gómez at (202) 512-3841 or gomezj@gao.gov.

What GAO Found

The Task Force agencies use the Action Plan to implement the Great Lakes Restoration Initiative (GLRI) and use an interagency process to enter into agreements among themselves to identify GLRI projects and with other stakeholders to implement GLRI projects. The Action Plan includes guidance for implementing the GLRI in five focus areas (such as invasive species and habitat and wildlife protection and restoration) that encompass the most significant environmental problems in the Great Lakes. Each focus area includes, among other things, long-term goals, objectives to be achieved by fiscal year 2014, and 28 measures of progress that have annual targets for fiscal years 2010 to 2014.

EPA uses the Action Plan's measures to assess GLRI progress. However, its methods may not produce comprehensive and useful assessments of GLRI progress for several reasons. Among them, some of the goals and objectives do not link to any measures and, as a result, it is unclear how EPA will be able to assess progress toward them. In addition, some measures track actions that may not lead to the desired GLRI goal. For example, one measure tracks the reduction in concentrations of polychlorinated biphenyls (PCB) in fish as part of the goal to lift all restrictions on consumption of Great Lakes fish. However, stakeholders reported that the measure is too narrow and that mercury and other contaminants need to be addressed as well. Consequently, reducing PCB concentrations in fish is not likely to lead to the desired result of lifting all Great Lakes fish consumption restrictions. Without useful measures, EPA may not be able to determine that GLRI efforts are producing the desired results.

In spring 2013, the Task Force agencies issued two reports about GLRI progress in fiscal years 2010 and 2011, which state whether the targets for the Action Plan's 28 measures were being met (e.g., 15 of 28 measures met or exceeded in fiscal year 2011), but the reports include few specific examples of progress. As a result, GAO sought further insights into such progress by surveying nonfederal GLRI stakeholders. Overall, 87 percent of respondents cited at least one example of how one or more of their projects had, or was expected to, benefit the Great Lakes ecosystem. GAO and others have reported that quantifying overall Great Lakes restoration progress is difficult, that the environmental conditions of each lake are unique, and, according to a 2006 U.N. report, it is often impossible to attribute specific environmental changes to specific projects or programs.

In response to GAO's survey, among the factors respondents most often cited as potentially limiting GLRI progress are several outside the scope of the Action Plan, such as inadequate infrastructure for wastewater or stormwater and the effects of climate change. These factors could negatively affect GLRI restoration efforts. For example, as a result of climate change, warming water temperatures can lead to increased numbers of aquatic invasive species and a decline in native ones, a GLRI focus area. The Action Plan touches on these factors but does not state how they will be addressed. In 2012, EPA took steps to incorporate climate change considerations into a small number of GLRI projects but has yet to decide if the GLRI will consider climate change impacts on all GLRI projects. Without addressing these factors in the next Action Plan, EPA will not be able to more fully account for their impacts on GLRI restoration efforts.

_____ United States Government Accountability Office

Contents

Tables

Figures

Abbreviations

Action Plan	Great Lakes Restoration Initiative Action Plan
EPA	Environmental Protection Agency
GLAS	Great Lakes Accountability System
GLRI	Great Lakes Restoration Initiative
GPRA	Government Performance and Results Act of 1993
PCB	polychlorinated biphenyls
Task Force	Great Lakes Interagency Task Force

GAO U.S. GOVERNMENT ACCOUNTABILITY OFFICE

441 G St. N.W.
Washington, DC 20548

September 27, 2013

The Honorable Bill Shuster
Chairman
Committee on Transportation and Infrastructure
House of Representatives

The Honorable Bob Gibbs
Chairman
Subcommittee on Water Resources and Environment
Committee on Transportation and Infrastructure
House of Representatives

The Great Lakes form the largest system of freshwater on earth. They contain about 84 percent of North America's surface freshwater and are shared by eight U.S. states—Illinois, Indiana, Michigan, Minnesota, New York, Ohio, Pennsylvania, and Wisconsin—the Canadian province of Ontario, and more than 40 tribes. The Great Lakes provide a variety of recreational, environmental, and economic benefits, including drinking water, fishing, swimming, boating, agriculture, industry, and shipping, for the more than 30 million people who reside in the Great Lakes Basin, which includes the five Great Lakes and the large land area that extends beyond the lakes, including their watersheds, tributaries, and connecting channels. In addition, a 2011 Michigan Sea Grant study estimated that 1.5 million jobs in the United States were directly connected to the Great Lakes and generated $62 billion in wages in 2009.[1]

However, the Great Lakes face significant environmental and public health stresses that continue to threaten their future. For example, advisories that warn against the consumption of certain fish species have been issued for each of the Great Lakes states due to their levels of persistent toxic substances, such as mercury. Decades of industrial activity in the region have left a legacy of contamination, such as from polychlorinated biphenyls (PCB), that resulted in the United States and

---

[1]Lynn Vaccaro and Jennifer Read, *Vital to Our Nation's Economy: Great Lakes Jobs 2011 Report* (Michigan Sea Grant, 2011). Michigan Sea Grant funds scientific research, education, and extension projects designed to foster science-based decisions about the use and conservation of Great Lakes resources. Michigan Sea Grant also provides access to science-based information about Michigan's coasts and the Great Lakes.

GAO-13-797 Great Lakes Restoration Initiative

Canada identifying, since 1987, a list of 43 severely degraded locations in the Great Lakes Basin as areas of concern; 26 of these areas of concern are located wholly in the United States, and 5 are shared between the two nations. In addition, more than 180 nonnative or "invasive" aquatic species have become established in the Great Lakes. Some invasive species have caused extensive ecological and economic damage to the Great Lakes. The zebra mussel, for example, outcompetes native species for resources by removing live animals and algae that other fish eat from water bodies, and it blocks pipes that deliver drinking water to cities and cooling water to power plants. The Fish and Wildlife Service has estimated a potential economic impact of $5 billion from 2000 to 2010 within the Great Lakes Basin alone. The discovery of Asian carp near waterways connected to the lakes threatens to increase this problem.[2]

In response to these concerns, President Obama proposed $475 million in his fiscal year 2010 budget request for a new interagency initiative to accelerate the restoration of the Great Lakes. Specifically, the President requested that the U.S. Environmental Protection Agency (EPA) and its federal partners coordinate state, tribal, local, and industry actions to protect, maintain, and restore the integrity of the Great Lakes. The Department of the Interior Appropriations Act for fiscal year 2010 authorized EPA to transfer up to $475 million appropriated for the Great Lakes Initiative to any federal agency to carry out activities in support of the Great Lakes Restoration Initiative (GLRI).[3] The accompanying conference report directed EPA to develop a comprehensive, multiyear restoration action plan that includes targets and measurable objectives from fiscal years 2010 to 2014 that would lead to the restoration of the Great Lakes.[4] The conference report also directed EPA to provide detailed, yearly program accomplishments starting in 2011 and to develop a process that ensures monitoring and reporting on the progress of the

---

[2]The term Asian carp refers collectively to four species of carp—including bighead and silver carp—that are native to Asia and were first introduced into the United States in 1963. Their rapid expansion and population increase can decrease populations of native aquatic species, in part by consuming vast areas of aquatic plants that are important as food and spawning and nursery habitats.

[3]Pub. L. No. 111-88, 123 Stat. 2904, 2938 (2009). For additional information on the Great Lakes Initiative, see GAO, *Great Lakes Initiative: EPA Needs to Better Ensure the Complete and Consistent Implementation of Water Quality Standards*, GAO-05-829 (Washington, D.C.: July 27, 2005).

[4]H. R. Rep. No. 111-316, at 111 (2009).

GLRI. Nearly $300 million was appropriated in both fiscal years 2011 and 2012 for the GLRI and, according to EPA, about $284 million in fiscal year 2013, for a total of approximately $1.3 billion since fiscal year 2010.[5]

The Great Lakes Interagency Task Force (Task Force)—created in May 2004 by Executive Order 13340—oversees the GLRI.[6] The Task Force is chaired by the EPA Administrator, and it includes senior officials from the U.S. Departments of Agriculture, Commerce, Defense, Health and Human Services, Homeland Security, Housing and Urban Development, the Interior, State, and Transportation and the White House Council on Environmental Quality. The GLRI is implemented by EPA's Great Lakes National Program Office in conjunction with subagencies within the 11 Task Force agencies.[7] EPA and the other Task Force agencies issued the *Great Lakes Restoration Initiative Action Plan Fiscal Years 2010-2014* (Action Plan) in February 2010.[8] In addition, EPA created the Great Lakes Accountability System (GLAS) as a mechanism for collecting information to monitor GLRI projects and progress.

Both our work and that of EPA's Office of the Inspector General have documented concerns about Great Lakes restoration efforts in the past. For example, we reported in May 2002 that the pace of cleaning up the Great Lakes and restoring areas of concern was slower than anticipated

---

[5]The amounts appropriated are approximate because of across the board rescissions and other adjustments.

[6]Executive Order 13340, Establishment of Great Lakes Interagency Task Force and Promotion of a Regional Collaboration of National Significance for the Great Lakes, 69 Fed. Reg. 29043 (May 20, 2004).

[7]The subagencies within the Task Force agencies that are responsible for implementing the GLRI are: the Department of Agriculture's Animal and Plant Health Inspection Service, Forest Service, and Natural Resources Conservation Service; the Department of Commerce's National Oceanic and Atmospheric Administration; the Department of Defense's U.S. Army Corps of Engineers; the Department of Health and Human Services' Agency for Toxic Substances and Disease Registry; the Department of Homeland Security's Coast Guard; the Department of the Interior's Bureau of Indian Affairs, Fish and Wildlife Service, National Park Service, and U.S. Geological Survey; and the Department of Transportation's Federal Highway Administration and Maritime Administration. We refer to all 16 Task Force agencies and subagencies collectively as Task Force agencies in this report, as is the case on the GLRI website http://greatlakesrestoration.us/priorities.html.

[8]Great Lakes Interagency Task Force, *Great Lakes Restoration Initiative Action Plan Fiscal Years 2010-2014*, 09-P-0231 (Washington, D.C.: Feb. 21, 2010.)

by the United States and Canada.[9] In September 2004, we found that EPA monitoring efforts did not provide comprehensive information on the condition of the Great Lakes and that monitoring by other federal and state agencies yielded information that that did not cover all areas related to the condition of the Great Lakes or the entire Great Lakes Basin.[10] In September 2009, EPA's Office of the Inspector General reported that EPA had not developed an effective management framework to clean up contaminated sediments in the Great Lakes areas of concern.[11]

In light of these past issues and the significant federal funds targeted toward addressing Great Lakes issues, you asked us to review the GLRI. This report examines (1) how the GLRI is implemented by the Task Force agencies and other stakeholders; (2) the methods that EPA has in place to assess GLRI progress; (3) the progress identified by the Task Force agencies and nonfederal stakeholders; and (4) the views of nonfederal stakeholders on factors, if any, that may affect or limit GLRI progress.

To examine how Task Force agencies and other stakeholders implement the GLRI and identify methods that EPA has in place to assess GLRI progress, we analyzed key documents including the Action Plan, EPA's GLRI financial reports, and information about GLRI projects from GLAS. In addition, we interviewed federal stakeholders—officials from each Task Force agency and relevant subagencies responsible for implementing the GLRI—and nonfederal stakeholders; specifically, representatives from state and local governments, tribes, nongovernmental organizations—such as the Nature Conservancy and the Great Lakes Indian Fish and Wildlife Commission—and academic institutions that that have received GLRI funds to gain an understanding of the GLRI and how it is

---

[9]GAO, *Great Lakes: EPA Needs to Define Organizational Responsibilities Better for Effective Oversight and Cleanup of Contaminated Areas*, GAO-02-563 (Washington, D.C.: May 17, 2002). No area of concern had had its designation removed—that is, been delisted—by May 17, 2002. EPA has since delisted two areas of concern, one before the creation of the GLRI, in 2006, and one after the creation of the GLRI, in 2013.

[10]GAO, *Great Lakes: Organizational Leadership and Restoration Goals Need to Be Better Defined for Monitoring Restoration Progress*, GAO-04-1024 (Washington, D.C.: Sept. 28, 2004).

[11]EPA Office of the Inspector General, *EPA Needs a Cohesive Plan to Clean Up the Great Lakes Areas of Concern* (Washington, D.C.: Sept. 14, 2009).

implemented.[12] We also interviewed representatives from a prominent Great Lakes interest group, the Healing Our Waters – Great Lakes Coalition, that has not received GLRI funds. We visited GLRI projects, and attended the Eighth Annual Great Lakes Restoration Conference in Cleveland in September 2012. In addition, we interviewed a nonprobability sample of 21 individuals with expertise in Great Lakes' subject matter to obtain their views about the Action Plan and Great Lakes restoration. The 21 subject matter experts who participated in these interviews included officials from state agencies, members of academia, and nongovernmental organizations. We selected these experts in part through recommendations made by nonfederal attendees at the Great Lakes Restoration Conference. Because we used a nonprobability sample, the information obtained from these interviews is not generalizable to other individuals with Great Lakes-related expertise but provides illustrative information.

To examine the progress identified by the Task Force agencies and nonfederal stakeholders and the views of nonfederal stakeholders on factors, if any, that may affect or limit GLRI progress, we reviewed key documents detailing Great Lakes restoration efforts. We also administered a web-based survey to each of the 205 nonfederal stakeholders that, as of October 2012, had received GLRI funds from a Task Force agency and had a project identified in GLAS. We conducted this survey to identify examples of GLRI progress and obtain stakeholder views on factors that might limit progress. Of the 205 stakeholders contacted, 176 completed the survey, for an overall response rate of 86 percent. We also asked the 21 subject matter experts we interviewed to provide their views about factors that may limit GLRI progress. Appendix I presents a more detailed description of our objectives, scope, and methodology.

We conducted this performance audit from June 2012 to September 2013 in accordance with generally accepted government auditing standards. Those standards require that we plan and perform the audit to obtain sufficient, appropriate evidence to provide a reasonable basis for our findings and conclusions based on our audit objectives. We believe that

---

[12]We did not include the Department of Housing and Urban Development because officials from that agency and EPA told us that it has not been involved with the Task Force or the GLRI.

the evidence obtained provides a reasonable basis for our findings and conclusions based on our audit objectives.

Background

The Great Lakes Basin spans more than 750 miles from east to west and, as shown in figure 1, encompasses nearly all of Michigan, and parts of Illinois, Indiana, Minnesota, New York, Ohio, Pennsylvania, Wisconsin, and Ontario, Canada. The U.S. shoreline along the five Great Lakes—Erie, Huron, Michigan, Ontario, and Superior—is approximately 4,530 miles long, which is more than 2,000 miles longer than the U.S. coastline on the Atlantic Ocean.

Figure 1: Area Comprising the Great Lakes Basin

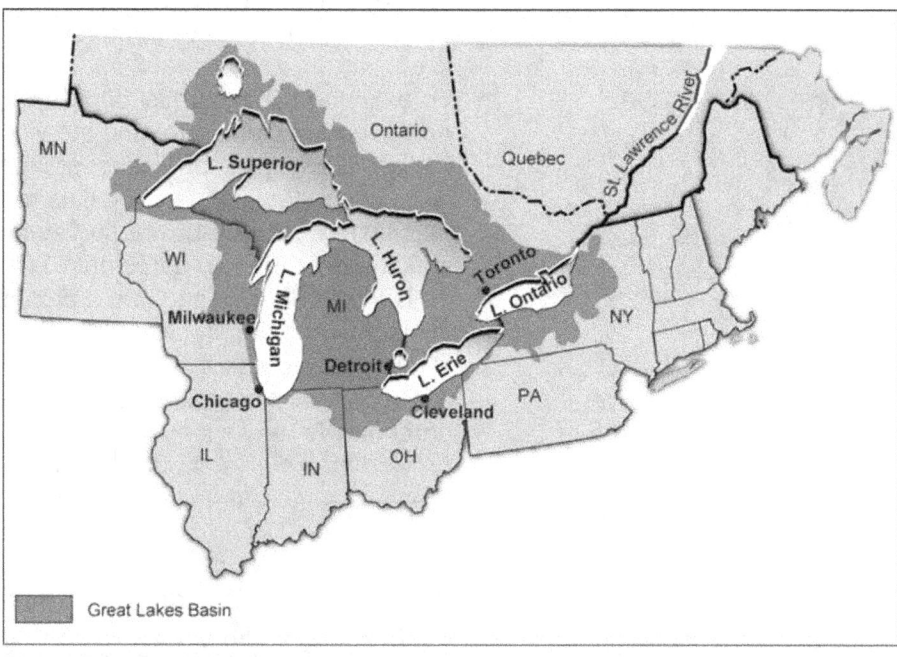

Great Lakes Basin

Sources: GAO, Map Resources (map).

Numerous stresses threaten the health of the lakes themselves and the adjacent land within the Great Lakes Basin. For example, Asian carp threaten commercial and recreational fisheries in the Great Lakes because they tend to outcompete native fish for resources and modify habitat. In addition, despite progress in reducing the amount of phosphorus in the lakes achieved through mitigation techniques implemented in the 1970s, harmful algal blooms are once again threatening the Great Lakes Basin.[13]

The United States has taken several steps to restore the health of the Great Lakes ecosystem during the last four decades. Examples are as follows:

- In 1972, the United States and Canada signed the first binational Great Lakes Water Quality Agreement with the goal of restoring and maintaining the chemical, physical, and biological integrity of the Great Lakes Basin. The parties signed another Great Lakes Water Quality Agreement in 1978 that was amended in 1983, 1987, and in 2012. The 1987 amendment resulted in the formal identification of specific areas of concern, which were defined as geographic areas where a change in the chemical, physical, or biological integrity of the area is sufficient to cause restrictions on fish and wildlife or drinking water consumption, or the loss of fish and wildlife habitat, among other conditions, or impair the area's ability to support aquatic life.[14] The 2012 amendment contains provisions for addressing the nearshore environment, [15] aquatic invasive species, habitat degradation, and the effects of climate change, among other things.

- In 2002, the Great Lakes Legacy Act authorized EPA to, among other things, carry out sediment remediation projects and to conduct sediment contamination remediation research in areas of concern in the Great Lakes.[16]

---

[13]According to EPA, phosphorus is a nutrient that controls the amount of algae that will grow suspended in water, and increases in phosphorus can result in increases in algae, which can be detrimental to aquatic life by reducing the amount of available oxygen and sunlight, among other things.

[14]For a complete list of area of concern conditions, click http://www.ijc.org/rel/boards/annex2/buis.htm.

[15]The aquatic nearshore can be considered to begin at the shoreline and extend offshore to the depth at which the warm surface waters typically reach the bottom in early fall, generally 20 to 30 meters deep (i.e., 65 feet 7.4 inches to 98 feet 5.1 inches). Terrestrial nearshore areas range from narrow beaches to inland features affected by lake water.

[16]Pub. L. No. 107-303, 116 Stat. 2355 (2002). Congress consolidated funding for the Great Lakes Legacy Act under the GLRI in 2009. *See* H. R. Rep. No. 111-316, at 110 (2009).

- In 2004, the Task Force agencies collaborated with Great Lakes governors, mayors, tribes, and nongovernmental organizations in an effort referred to as the Great Lakes Regional Collaboration, which led to the development in 2005 of the *Great Lakes Regional Collaboration Strategy to Restore and Protect the Great Lakes.*[17] More than 1,500 individuals participated in this effort. A 2007 Brookings Institution report estimated that the $26 billion dollar investment necessary to implement this strategy would have resulted in $30 to $50 billion in short-term benefits to the regional economy and at least $50 billion in the long term.[18]

Even with these actions, the Great Lakes are environmentally vulnerable. In 2009, the President requested and Congress appropriated $475 million for fiscal year 2010 to create the GLRI. The accompanying conference report directed EPA to develop a GLRI Action Plan and to ensure that the GLRI funds supplement and expand, not supplant, federal agency Great Lakes programs.[19] EPA and the Task Force agencies issued the Action Plan in February 2010 to guide the implementation of the GLRI. According to the Action Plan, the GLRI is intended to build on previous restoration strategies to develop a collaborative approach to restoring the health of the Great Lakes ecosystem. The conference report also directed EPA to engage an independent, scientific panel to review the scientific credibility of the plan to optimize the likelihood of successful restoration at appropriate scales.[20] In response, EPA engaged its Science Advisory Board to conduct a review of the Action Plan.[21] Among other things, the Science Advisory Board recommended that EPA take steps to develop an

---

[17]Great Lakes Regional Collaboration, *Great Lakes Regional Collaboration Strategy to Restore and Protect the Great Lakes* (December 2005).

[18]Austin et al., *Healthy Waters, Strong Economy: The Benefits of Restoring the Great Lakes Ecosystem* (Washington, D.C.: The Brookings Institution, September 2007).

[19]H. R. Rep. No. 111-316, at 110-11 (2009).

[20]H. R. Rep. No. 111-316, at 111 (2009).

[21]A 1977 law required EPA to establish a Science Advisory Board to provide scientific advice on a variety of matters. The board, which is a federal advisory committee, has established several standing committees, including the Ecological Processes and Effects Committee.

adaptive management framework for the GLRI and noted that EPA should consider potential impacts of climate change on restoration.[22]

In March 2013, the Chair of the Council on Environmental Quality announced that the administration is committing to another 5-year GLRI Action Plan, for fiscal years 2015 to 2019. In May 2013, EPA and the Task Force agencies began conducting public meetings and webinars to obtain comments on how the Action Plan could be refined to increase the effectiveness of GLRI investments during the next phase of the Action Plan.

Task Force Agencies Use the Action Plan and Agreements among Themselves and with Nonfederal Stakeholders to Implement the GLRI

The Task Force agencies use the Action Plan to guide implementation of the GLRI. They also use an interagency process to identify and transfer funds to GLRI work, and to enter into agreements among themselves and with nonfederal stakeholders to identify and implement GLRI projects, or they do the work themselves.

Task Force Agencies Use the Action Plan to Implement the GLRI

The Task Force agencies use the Action Plan to guide implementation of the GLRI. The Action Plan is organized into five focus areas that, according to the Task Force agencies, encompass the most significant environmental problems in the Great Lakes: (1) toxic substances and areas of concern; (2) invasive species; (3) nearshore health and nonpoint source pollution; (4) habitat and wildlife protection and restoration; and (5) accountability, education, monitoring, evaluation, communication, and partnerships. Table 1 describes each focus area.

---

[22]EPA Science Advisory Board, *Review of Great Lakes Restoration Initiative Action Plan* (Washington, D.C.: Jan. 24, 2012).

Table 1: Descriptions of the Five Great Lakes Restoration Initiative Action Plan Focus Areas

Focus area	Description
Toxic substances and areas of concern	Includes pollution prevention and cleanup of the most polluted areas in the Great Lakes
Invasive species	Includes efforts to institute a "zero tolerance policy" toward new invasions of non-native species, such as Asian carp
Nearshore health and nonpoint source pollution	Includes targeted geographic focus on high-priority watersheds and reducing polluted runoff from urban, suburban, and agricultural sources
Habitat and wildlife protection and restoration	Includes revitalizing wetlands and other habitat, and a comprehensive assessment of the entire Great Lakes coastal wetlands for the purpose of strategically targeting restoration and protection efforts in a science-based manner
Accountability, education, monitoring, evaluation, communication, and partnerships	Includes the implementation of goal- and results-based accountability measures, learning initiatives, outreach, and strategic partnerships

Source: GAO analysis of Great Lakes Restoration Initiative Action Plan.

Each focus area includes a description of its stresses and several long-term goals to address them. For example, one long-term goal in the invasive species focus area is to eliminate the introduction of new invasive species to the Great Lakes Basin. In addition, each focus area includes a number of objectives to be completed within the 5-year period covered by the Action Plan. For example, in the habitat and wildlife protection and restoration focus area, one objective is to assess 100 percent of U.S. coastal wetlands in the Great Lakes Basin by 2014.

The focus areas also include measures of progress—28 in total—each of which has annual targets for fiscal years 2010 to 2014 that are designed to ensure that efforts are on track to meet the long-term goals. Some of the measures address environmental conditions. For example, one measure for the habitat and wildlife protection and restoration focus area addresses the number of fish passage barriers that are to be removed or bypassed annually for the period of time covered by the Action Plan. The annual targets for the measure are the removal or bypassing of 100 barriers in 2010, 150 in 2011, 250 in 2012, 350 in 2013, and 450 barriers in 2014.

The last part of each focus area is the principal actions, broad statements of the most significant activities that EPA and its federal partners conclude need to be done in order to achieve the goals, objectives, and targets in the Action Plan. For example, a principal action for the invasive species focus area is to promote the development and use of new control technologies, including biological control methods, that will significantly reduce the cost or increase the effectiveness of invasive species control measures.

See appendix VI for a complete list of the Action Plan long-term goals, objectives, and measures of progress.

Task Force Agencies Use Interagency Process to Identify and Fund GLRI Work

The Task Force agencies identify the GLRI projects they plan to implement through an interagency process. EPA and the other Task Force agencies then enter into interagency agreements that describe the scope of the GLRI work that is to be undertaken and the amount of GLRI funds EPA will transfer to the Task Force agency doing that work.

The Task Force agencies and nonfederal stakeholders have started more than 1,450 GLRI projects since the program began.[23] GLRI projects can range in size from 0.25 acres for a fish spawning project to 10 million acres for a project to update habitat and wetland maps to identify sensitive and restorable wetlands across the basin. These projects may take place in one location or across multiple states within the Great Lakes Basin. GLRI projects have also ranged in cost from $3,000 to protect nesting piping plovers to $60.5 million to address contaminated sediment in multiple areas of concern.[24] Many GLRI projects take several years to complete and, as a result, many projects funded in fiscal years 2010 to 2012 are still under way. For example, approximately 64 percent of the fiscal year 2010 to 2012 projects reported in GLAS were at least half completed as of May 2013. Tables 2 and 3 show the number of projects

---

[23]For the purpose of this report, we are counting only those projects that were identified in GLAS in May 2013. It is the case that some projects identified in GLAS comprise multiple efforts that are reported as a greater number of separate projects at the GLRI website, http://glri.us/projects/index.html. According to an EPA official, some Task Force agencies may report these individual efforts on the website to provide more comprehensive information on GLRI activities to the public. In May 2013, there were 1,534 GLRI projects identified on the website.

[24]The piping plover is a small shore bird that uses open sandy beaches for its habitat. The piping plover in the Great Lakes watershed was listed as endangered under the Endangered Species Act in 1985.

funded by Task Force agency and by focus area as of May 2013, respectively.[25]

Table 2: Number of Great Lakes Restoration Initiative Projects Funded by Task Force Agencies Reported in the Great Lakes Accountability System as of May 2013

Agency	Subagency	Number of projects
Environmental Protection Agency		498
Department of the Interior	Fish and Wildlife Service	379
	U.S. Geological Survey	75
	Bureau of Indian Affairs	33
	National Park Service	31
Department of Defense	U.S. Army Corps of Engineers	244
Department of Commerce	National Oceanic and Atmospheric Administration	113
Department of Agriculture	Forest Service	37
	Natural Resources Conservation Service	18
	Animal and Plant Health Inspection Service	18
Department of Homeland Security	U.S. Coast Guard	19
Department of Transportation	Federal Highway Administration	7
	Maritime Administration	4
Department of Health and Human Services	Agency for Toxic Substances and Disease Registry	5
Council on Environmental Quality		2
Total		**1,483**

Source: GAO analysis of EPA data.

[25]The total number of GLRI projects identified by Task Force agency in table 2, 1,483, is less than the number of GLRI projects identified by focus area in table 3, 1,487, because 4 GLRI projects are funded by two federal subagencies that were not identified as Task Force agencies and, therefore, are not included in table 2. These subagencies are the Department of Agriculture's Cooperative State Research, Education, and Extension Service and the Department of Health and Human Service's Federal Occupational Health.

GAO-13-797 Great Lakes Restoration Initiative

Table 3: Number of Great Lakes Restoration Initiative Projects by Focus Area Reported in the Great Lakes Accountability System as of May 2013

Focus area	Number of projects
Toxic substances and areas of concern	235
Invasive species	192
Nearshore health and nonpoint source pollution	247
Habitat and wildlife protection and restoration	630
Accountability, education, monitoring, evaluation, communication, and partnerships	183
Total	**1,487**

Source: GAO analysis of EPA data.

Although we did not break down GLRI funding per project in detail, some Task Force agency officials told us that they use a small percentage of that funding for administrative tasks. For example, officials from one Task Force agency told us that they used 5 percent of GLRI funds for one agency project for overhead and indirect costs. In this case, the agency performs laboratory and monitoring work that the nonfederal stakeholders that implement the project do not have the capacity to do. As shown in figures 2 and 3, most GLRI funding has been utilized by EPA, the Department of the Interior's Fish and Wildlife Service, and the U.S. Army Corps of Engineers, and focus area one—toxic substances and areas of concern—has received more GLRI funding than the other focus areas in each of the past 4 years.

Figure 2: Great Lakes Restoration Initiative Allocations by Agency in Fiscal Years 2010 through 2013 as of April 2013

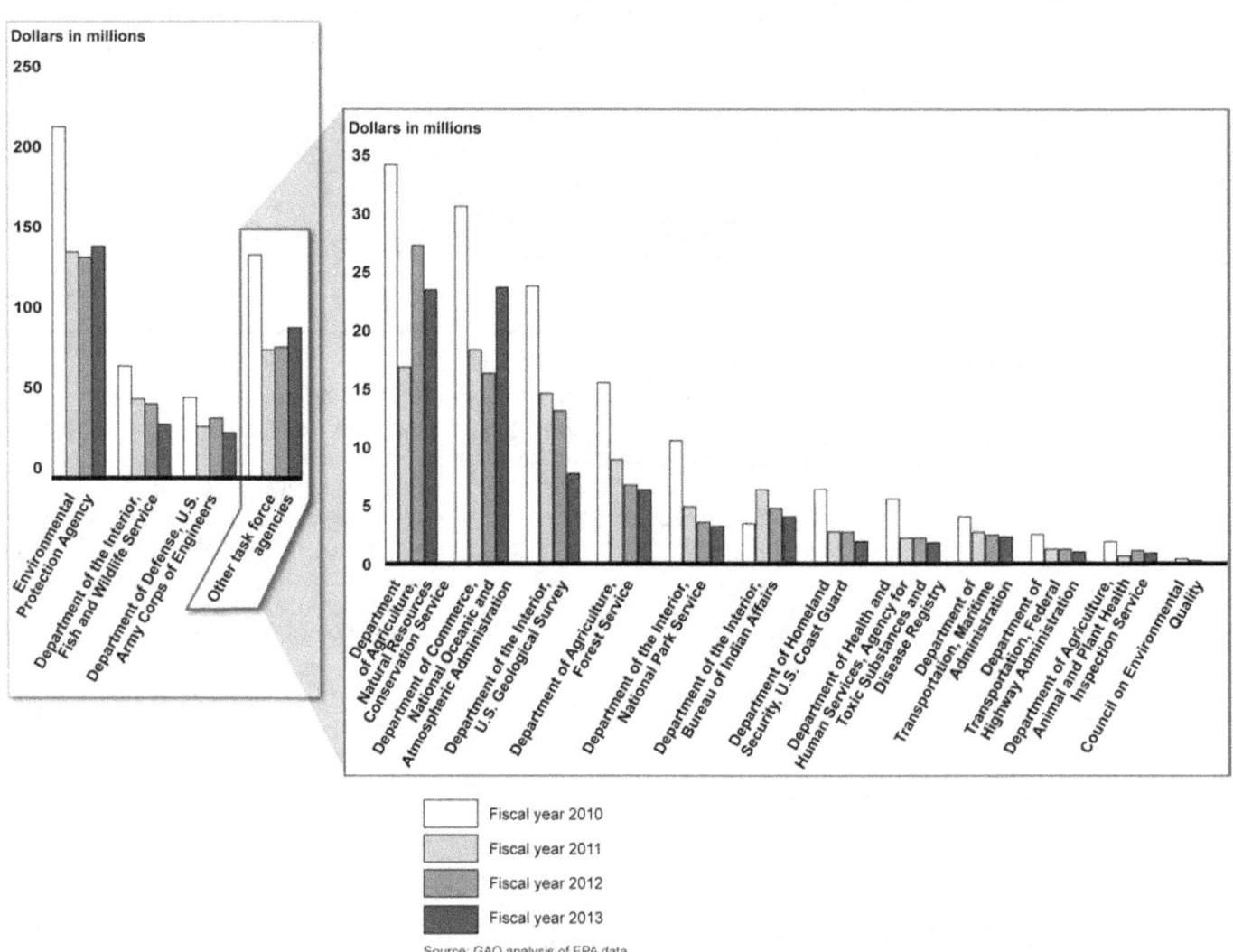

Source: GAO analysis of EPA data.

Note: In addition to funding Great Lakes Restoration Initiative (GLRI) projects, EPA uses its GLRI funds for, among other things, Great Lakes Legacy Act projects and GLRI funding for the Great Lakes Fishery Commission and International Joint Commission. The Great Lakes Fishery Commission and International Joint Commission are binational efforts supported by the Department of State. The Great Lakes Fishery Commission works to sustain productivity of fish stocks of U.S. and Canadian concern in the Great Lakes, among other things, and the International Joint Commission assists the United States and Canada in the protection of the transboundary environment in part through the implementation of the Great Lakes Water Quality Agreement, among other things.

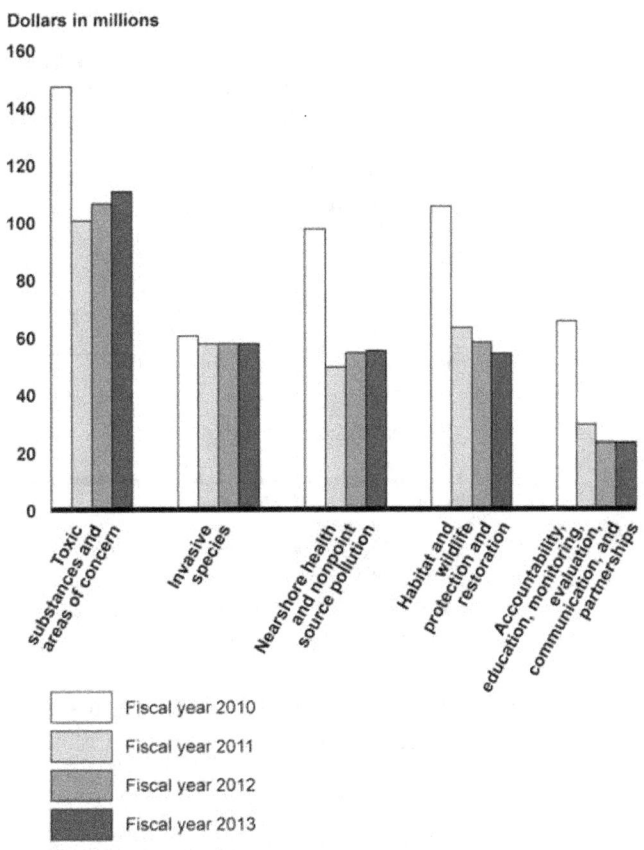

Figure 3: Great Lakes Restoration Initiative Allocations by Focus Area in Fiscal Years 2010 through 2013 as of April 2013

Dollars in millions

Fiscal year 2010
Fiscal year 2011
Fiscal year 2012
Fiscal year 2013

Source: GAO analysis of EPA data.

EPA and the Task Force agencies have 2 years to obligate GLRI funds, which means that the amounts allocated in fiscal years 2010 and 2011 are not likely to change, but fiscal year 2012 and 2013 amounts may change as the period for obligating those funds comes to an end. In addition, while nearly all of the GLRI appropriations from fiscal years 2010 to 2012 have been obligated, not all of those obligations have been outlayed because many GLRI projects take several years to complete.[26] Table 4 shows the extent to which GLRI appropriations for fiscal years 2010 to 2012 have been obligated and outlayed as of July 2013.

Table 4: Percentage of Great Lakes Restoration Initiative Appropriations Allocated, Obligated, and Outlayed for Fiscal Years 2010 through 2012, as of July 2013

Dollar in millions

Appropriations allocated, obligated, and outlayed	Fiscal year 2010	Fiscal year 2011	Fiscal year 2012
Appropriations	$475	$300	$300
Percentage of appropriations allocated	100%	99.8%	99.84%
Percentage of appropriations obligated	99.74%	99.74%	98.42%
Percentage of appropriations outlayed	79.53%	63.12%	28.17%

Source: GAO analysis of EPA information.

Note: Appropriation amounts are approximate and do not reflect across the board rescissions and other adjustments.

After EPA and the Task Force agencies have agreed to the GLRI fund transfers to each agency and the work that will be done, each agency either does the work itself or implements it through mechanisms such as cooperative agreements, contracts, or grants with nonfederal stakeholders. In the case of GLRI grants, a Task Force agency announces the availability of the grants through a request for application process. For example, EPA announced on April 19, 2012, that the agency planned to award approximately $20 million for about 100 projects in four

---

[26]Appropriations represent budget authority to incur obligations and make payments from the U.S. Treasury for specified purposes. For budgeting purposes, an allocation means an authorized delegation by one agency of its authority to obligate budget authority and outlay funds to another agency, and it is made when one or more agencies share the administration of a program for which appropriations are made to only one of the agencies. For funds controls purpose, an allocation is a subdivision of an apportionment, which divides the amount available for obligation in an appropriation. Obligations are definite commitments that create a legal liability of the government for the payment of goods and services ordered or received, or a legal duty on the part of the United States that could mature into a legal liability by virtue of actions on the part of the other party beyond the control of the United States. Outlays are the issuance of checks, disbursement of cash, or electronic transfer of funds made to liquidate a federal obligation. See GAO, *A Glossary of Terms Used in the Federal Budget Process*, GAO-05-734SP (Washington, D.C.: Sept. 1, 2005).

of the five focus areas, and that the applications were due on May 24, 2012.[27] The request for application document included the amount of money and number of grants that would be awarded in each focus area and grant eligibility information, among other things. Similar announcements were made by other Task Force agencies for their GLRI grants, and EPA issued its first request for applications for fiscal year 2013 projects in July 2013.

EPA's Methods to Assess GLRI Progress May Not Produce Comprehensive and Useful Assessments or Support Program Adjustments

Although EPA uses information from GLAS and a variety of other sources to assess GLRI progress in meeting the annual targets associated with each of the 28 measures of progress in the Action Plan to assess GLRI progress, this information may not produce sufficiently comprehensive or useful assessments or support program adjustments. Specifically, (1) the Action Plan measures of progress currently in place may not provide sufficiently comprehensive or useful information and (2) EPA and the Task Force agencies have not fully established a plan to guide an adaptive management process for the GLRI that could allow them to assess the effectiveness of GLRI actions and, if needed, adjust their efforts.

EPA Uses the Action Plan Measures to Assess GLRI Progress

EPA assesses GLRI progress primarily by evaluating performance toward meeting the annual targets for the 28 measures of progress in the Action Plan, which EPA officials said are intended as indicators of success for each focus area. Of the 28 measures, 15 are also used in the agency's performance plan and performance report, which are required by the Government Performance and Results Act of 1993 (GPRA) as amended.[28] According to EPA officials, the agency sought to develop, in consultation with the Office of Management and Budget, a limited set of measures that could be used to evaluate GLRI progress on an annual

---

[27]EPA did not request applications for grants in the habitat and wildlife protection and restoration focus area in the agency's April 19, 2012, request for applications, noting that the National Oceanic and Atmospheric Administration and Fish and Wildlife Service would be requesting grants in that area that year.

[28]Pub. L. No. 103-62 (1993), *amended by* GPRA Modernization Act of 2010, Pub. L. No. 111-352 (2011). GPRA sought to improve the effectiveness and accountability of federal programs by requiring federal agencies to set goals for program performance, measure results, and report on annual performance compared with the goals. GPRA as amended requires, among other things, that federal agencies develop strategic plans.

basis. EPA officials said that, in developing the set of measures, they considered such factors as the availability of relevant data, the suitability of the data for measuring year-to-year changes, a focus on environmental outcomes, and the existing federal authorities available to address the measure. Officials from EPA and another Task Force agency also told us that many of the measures were based on existing baseline information and were practical because they used existing agency databases for information.

To gauge GLRI progress toward meeting the targets for the measures, EPA obtains the data needed using information from GLAS, EPA programs, other federal agencies, states, and universities. For example, for 7 of the 28 measures of progress, GLAS provides progress data specific to individual GLRI projects. In addition, states provide information on progress at areas of concern, the National Oceanic and Atmospheric Administration provides progress information from a database it manages on invasive species in the Great Lakes, and the Fish and Wildlife Service provides progress information related to habitat and wildlife protection and restoration. In March 2013, the Task Force agencies issued the first GLRI progress report to Congress, which identified fiscal year 2011 progress using the measures for each focus area and described the accomplishments of some projects.[29] The Task Force agencies also issued a report on fiscal year 2010 progress in April 2013.[30]

Action Plan Measures of Progress May Not Provide Sufficiently Comprehensive or Useful Information

Assessments of GLRI progress could help GLRI stakeholders, Congress, and the public discern the extent to which the health of the Great Lakes ecosystem has been restored, as well as what has been achieved by the approximately $1.3 billion appropriated to the program since fiscal year 2010. However, the Action Plan measures of progress may not provide sufficiently comprehensive or useful information on GLRI progress because (1) some goals and objectives do not link to any measures that will allow EPA to assess progress toward achieving them; (2) the measures do not capture the results of many of the GLRI projects; (3)

---

[29]EPA in partnership with the Great Lakes Interagency Task Force, *Great Lakes Restoration Initiative Fiscal Year 2011 Report to Congress and the President* (Washington, D.C.: September 2011).

[30]EPA in partnership with the Great Lakes Interagency Task Force, *Great Lakes Restoration Initiative Fiscal Year 2010 Report to Congress and the President* (Washington, D.C.: March 2011).

data used to evaluate some measures of progress may not be complete; and (4) some Task Force and state agency officials, subject matter experts, and EPA's Science Advisory Board raised concerns about the usefulness of some measures or their targets for indicating progress toward the GLRI goals and objectives.

Some GLRI Goals and Objectives Do Not Link to Any Measures

The Action Plan does not identify the links between a focus area's goals, objectives, and measures. Specifically, based on our analysis of the GLRI Action Plan, some of the goals and objectives in the Action Plan do not link to any measures of progress, which EPA uses to assess GLRI progress. For example, one of the goals of the habitat and wildlife protection and restoration focus area is that development activities are planned and implemented in ways that are sensitive to environmental considerations and compatible with fish and wildlife and their habitats. However, we found that none of the six objectives and nine measures of progress in this focus area link to this goal. Similarly, in its 2012 review of the GLRI Action Plan, EPA's Science Advisory Board commented on the ambiguity in the links between the elements of the plan, such as between the long-term goals and the objectives. The Science Advisory Board also recommended that the Action Plan tie the measures more directly to the goals, noting that the more clear and transparent the connection between the measures and the goals, the easier it will be to document how well the actions are working to meet the goals.

EPA officials told us that the Action Plan was not intended to contain direct linkages between every goal, objective, and measure but rather that the measures were to serve as key indicators of success for each focus area. They said that the rationale for that decision was to provide some flexibility, recognizing that not all important restoration work may fall within the measures of progress and that the Action Plan does not represent the entirety of actions necessary for Great Lakes protection and restoration. However, based on our review of documents on planning for restoration of natural resources, we believe that clear linkages between a plan's goals, objectives, and measures are critical to achieving and assessing progress over time. For example, the National Research Council recommended such linkages in its checklist for planning and evaluating aquatic ecosystem restoration.[31] Specifically, the National Research Council recommended constructing specific performance indicators that are directly and appropriately linked to each objective, noting that these performance indicators are specific, measureable quantities that reveal to what extent the objectives are being achieved.[32] In addition, the Department of the Interior's 2009 technical guidance on managing natural resources emphasizes that, to be useful for decision making and evaluation, objectives need to be unambiguous, with specific metrics and specific target conditions.[33]

We recognize that it may not always be feasible or appropriate to identify measures for every aspect of each goal or objective. Nonetheless, although some objectives in the Action Plan describe quantifiable actions, the Action Plan contains no measures of progress for them. For example, two Action Plan objectives for the nearshore health and nonpoint source pollution focus area state that, by 2014, (1) 50 percent of high priority Great Lakes beaches will have been assessed using a standardized sanitary survey tool to identify sources of contamination and (2) rapid testing or predictive modeling methods (i.e., to improve the accuracy of decisions on beach postings to better protect public health) will be employed at 33 percent of high-priority beaches. However, because the Action Plan contains no measures of progress that link to these objectives, it is unclear how EPA will be able to assess annual progress toward these and other objectives that do not have linked measures. EPA officials told us that they recognize the need to report a more comprehensive assessment of objectives and are considering options for evaluating and reporting on them.

---

[31]The National Research Council is the operating arm of the National Academy of Sciences and National Academy of Engineering. Its mission is to improve government decision making and public policy, increase public understanding, and promote the acquisition and dissemination of knowledge in matters involving science, engineering, technology, and health. For more information about the National Research Council click http://www.nationalacademies.org/nrc/index.html.

[32]National Research Council of the National Academies, Committee on Restoration of Aquatic Ecosystems: Science, Technology, and Public Policy, *Restoration of Aquatic Ecosystems: Science, Technology, and Public Policy* (Washington, D.C.: National Academies Press, 1992).

[33]B. K. Williams, R. C. Szaro, and C. D. Shapiro, *Adaptive Management: The U.S. Department of the Interior Technical Guide,* Adaptive Management Working Group, U.S. Department of the Interior (Washington, D.C.: 2009).

Measures Do Not Capture the Results of Many GLRI Projects

Many of the projects funded by the GLRI do not have an Action Plan measure of progress assigned to them, which means that the results of those projects are not captured by the measures. Specifically, nearly 60 percent of the more than 1,450 GLRI projects reported in GLAS as of May 2013 did not have an associated Action Plan measure of progress. One reason for this is that, according to a Task Force agency, some projects contribute to the Action Plan measures but are not the type of on-the-ground restoration projects that are addressed by most of the measures of progress. Officials from the U.S. Geological Survey told us that this is the case for much of their agency's GLRI work. For example, the agency's work has included efforts to develop new methods of controlling phragmites, an invasive plant.[34] This work contributes toward the Action Plan's objective of developing or refining and pilot testing five technologies to contain or control invasive species by 2014. However, there is no linked measure of progress for this objective or assigned to the project. As a result, EPA's progress assessments may inaccurately capture the extent of progress being made toward containing or controlling invasive species.

According to EPA officials, projects without assigned measures address the Action Plan goals, objectives, or principal actions; the reason these projects do not have measures assigned to them is that they do not directly provide data for any of the Action Plan's 28 measures. They told us that they monitor the results of individual projects through standard agency practices, but that they are not currently tracking cumulative results that are not addressed by an Action Plan measure of progress. According to agency officials, future GLRI progress assessments may capture more information. Specifically, they said that the cumulative results of some of the projects without assigned measures of progress may ultimately be captured by some of the existing measures. We recognize that this may be the case for some projects. For example, projects to restore native fish habitat that do not have assigned measures of progress could help lead to progress over time toward the measure that addresses the percentage of native aquatic species populations that are self-sustaining in the wild. However, a cumulative approach may not allow EPA to capture specific progress information from those projects

---

[34]*Phragmites australis*, or common reed, is a perennial grass now common in North American wetlands. Invasive phragmites create tall, dense stands that degrade wetlands and coastal areas by crowding out native plants and animals, blocking shoreline views, and reducing access for swimming, fishing, and hunting.

without measures, and EPA uses the measures to assess GLRI progress and has been directed to report on that progress annually. As we reported in November 2002, one attribute of successful performance assessment is that there should be enough measures to ensure that an agency has the information it needs about project performance.[35] Without methods to include the results of such projects, EPA cannot ensure that the agency is assessing the full extent of progress being made.

Data Used to Evaluate Some Measures of Progress May Not Be Complete

Data used to evaluate some measures of progress may not be complete because GLAS users are limited to reporting progress using a single measure, and GLRI projects may directly address multiple measures across different focus areas. We found that 7 of the 28 measures of progress are tracked primarily in GLAS and, as we noted previously, EPA uses information from GLAS, as well as other sources, to gauge GLRI progress toward meeting the targets for the measures. Officials from five Task Force agencies told us that this is a significant limitation that can result in underreporting of progress. For example, a National Park Service GLRI project has involved managing acres for invasive species, which is one measure, as well as outreach to the public on practices that prevent the introduction and spread of invasive species, which is another measure. However, GLAS requires the agency to choose only one of these measures for reporting progress. EPA officials told us that GLAS users are restricted to reporting on a single measure due primarily to a decision by EPA to simplify the reporting process during the initial stages of the GLRI. Agency officials said that this decision was made for several reasons, including concerns about double-counting and overreporting, a desire to minimize the reporting burden for GLAS users and EPA, and the need to ensure appropriate data quality review before making the progress information public. They said that the current design of GLAS reflects this decision and that system modifications would be necessary to allow reporting on multiple measures. However, by limiting users to reporting information on only a single measure for each project, GLAS prevents EPA from collecting complete progress information on GLRI projects—that is, information on each of the measures addressed by GLRI projects. As we noted previously, there should be enough measures to ensure that an agency has the information it needs to assess project performance. Without collecting information about the multiple measures

---

[35]For information on attributes of successful performance measures, see GAO, *Tax Administration: IRS Needs to Further Refine Its Tax Filing Season Performance Measures*, GAO-03-143 (Washington, D.C.: Nov. 22, 2002).

affected by a project, the data EPA is using for certain measures of progress cannot be complete, and EPA is likely underreporting progress for these measures.

EPA officials told us that they began to address this issue in fiscal year 2012 for two complementary measures in the habitat and wildlife protection and restoration focus area, the miles of rivers reopened for fish passage, and the number of fish passage barriers removed or bypassed. Specifically, EPA has begun asking GLRI funding recipients reporting on one of these measures to indicate progress, if any, on the complementary measure. This effort will help EPA obtain more complete information on these two measures, but it does not address the broader reporting limitation in GLAS, which EPA officials told us may result in underreporting of progress for certain measures. EPA officials told us that they will consider addressing this limitation in GLAS, but they did not indicate a time frame for doing so.

In addition, although EPA officials told us that they have concerns about the quality of GLRI progress information in GLAS, they have not fully assessed the quality of that information, such as its completeness, accuracy, and consistency. As a result, the agency has not made this information available to the public. While practices required under GPRA, as amended, are required at the federal department or agency level, we have previously reported that these requirements can serve as leading practices for planning at lower levels within federal agencies, such as individual programs or initiatives.[36] Thus, EPA is not required to address requirements under GPRA, as amended, for GLAS, but by following them, the agency would be implementing leading practices. The GPRA Modernization Act of 2010 requires, among other things, that agency performance plans and reports describe how the agency ensures the reliability of the data used to measure progress toward its performance goals, including how it verifies and validates measured values of performance and compensates for any limitations to the data to reach the required level of accuracy.[37] Verification includes the assessment of data

---

[36]See, for example, GAO, *Environmental Justice: EPA Needs to Take Additional Actions to Help Ensure Effective Implementation*, GAO-12-77 (Washington, D.C.: Oct. 6, 2011).

[37]Pub. L. No. 111-352, §§ 3-4 (2011). Prior to this amendment, the Government Performance and Results Act of 1993 also required agency performance plans to describe the means to be used to verify and validate measured values of performance. Pub. L. No. 103-62, § 4(b) (1993).

completeness, accuracy, and consistency to ensure that the data will be of sufficient quality to document performance and support decision making.[38] In light of this and EPA's concerns about the quality of the GLRI progress data in GLAS, we also have concerns about the use of these data for measuring progress toward the Action Plan goals and objectives.

GLRI funding recipients are responsible for entering information about the progress of their GLRI projects directly into GLAS, and EPA has methods in place to review this information on a project-by-project basis. For example, EPA has developed a plan for managing the grants, interagency agreements, and contracts the agency awards for GLRI projects. According to agency officials, this plan synthesizes existing agency standards and policies and itemizes the activities to be undertaken by project officers and others to ensure an effective grant oversight process. Among other things, this plan specifies that, for interagency agreements, EPA officials who are GLRI project officers will review progress reports submitted by GLRI funding recipients and that the project officers will compare the information in those reports to the information entered in GLAS.[39] According to EPA officials, project officers for grants are also expected to compare information in progress reports with information in GLAS.

However, EPA officials noted that they believe there are overall consistency issues with the progress information grantees enter in GLAS, and that there could be underreporting of progress for certain measures when they are being achieved by a large number of projects or stakeholders. However, the officials told us that they have not yet taken steps to identify the progress information in GLAS that may be incomplete, incorrect, or inconsistently entered by GLRI funding recipients. As a result, EPA's ability to reliably assess progress toward the targets for the seven measures tracked primarily in GLAS is questionable. EPA officials told us that they recognize the need to improve GLAS and that they are beginning efforts to review the system, including assessing their data quality and review procedures and

---

[38]GAO, *Performance Plans: Selected Approaches for Verification and Validation of Agency Performance Information*, GAO-GGD-99-139 (Washington, D.C.: July 30, 1999).

[39]GLRI funding recipients are required to submit semiannual progress reports to EPA. According to EPA officials, they do not use these project reports to assess GLRI progress. This is because the progress reports are for administrative management purposes and not for reporting progress made toward the Action Plan measures.

identifying improvements. The officials noted that they are also considering whether GLAS is the right tool for the GLRI. EPA officials had not determined a time frame for this work as of June 2013.

Some Measures or Their Targets May Not Be Indicative of Progress

Some Task Force and state agency officials, subject matter experts, and EPA's Science Advisory Board, raised concerns that certain measures of progress or their targets may not be useful for indicating GLRI progress toward the Action Plan's goals and objectives.

Climatic factors may affect the usefulness of some measures. Five of the six measures of progress for the nearshore health and nonpoint source pollution focus area may not be useful for indicating GLRI progress over the short term toward the Action Plan's goals and objectives. Specifically, EPA officials and others have noted that these measures address environmental conditions that are influenced by climatic factors, such as precipitation and wind patterns. These factors make it difficult to identify whether the restoration efforts are having the desired effects. For example, one of the measures of progress in the Action Plan for this focus area tracks the square miles of harmful algal blooms in the Great Lakes. According to information from EPA officials, such algal blooms are influenced by climatic factors such as precipitation patterns, water temperature, and wind speed and direction. Officials from another Task Force agency also told us that because of factors such as weather that cannot be controlled, the extent of algal blooms in any given year is not directly related to the management actions being taken in the GLRI and, as a result, the measure is not useful for indicating GLRI progress toward the Action Plan's goals and objectives. EPA officials told us that, given the short period of time the GLRI has been under way, factors such as temperature and the amount and timing of precipitation are currently the primary factors affecting the extent of algal bloom. Officials also told us that, over the long term, management actions will lead to lower phosphorous levels, which will have a minimizing affect on the extent of such algal blooms. However, over the short term, this measure may not be useful for indicating GLRI progress toward the focus area's objective of significantly reducing the number and severity of incidences of harmful algal blooms by 2014. In addition, we have previously reported criteria for determining the extent to which an agency's performance plan provides a clear picture of intended performance, including that measures must clearly represent or be related to the performance they are trying to assess.[40] Therefore, measures that track conditions that are not directly related to management actions being taken may not be useful for indicating GLRI progress toward the Action Plan's goals and objectives. While we recognize that the Action Plan is not a performance plan, using criteria intended for performance plans is appropriate because EPA uses the Action Plan's measures of progress to assess GLRI progress as an agency would use the measures in a performance plan.

Some measures track actions that may not be sufficient to lead to the desired GLRI goals. For example, one of the goals for the toxic substances and areas of concern focus area is that environmental levels of toxic chemicals are reduced to the point that all restrictions on the consumption of Great Lakes fish can be lifted. A measure of progress that links to this goal tracks the long-term reduction in average concentrations of PCBs in Great Lakes fish. However, officials from two Task Force agencies and two state agencies, as well as five subject matter experts, reported that the measure's focus on PCBs is too narrow and that other contaminants, particularly mercury, need to be addressed as well. EPA's Science Advisory Board also noted this narrow focus in its 2012 review of the Action Plan. Mercury is important because, according to a 2011 binational study of mercury in the Great Lakes region, it has widely contaminated the region and has been responsible for fish consumption advisories in the eight Great Lakes states and the Canadian province of Ontario.[41] The study concluded that mercury, largely due to atmospheric emissions from coal-fired power plants, remains a pollutant of major concern with an impact on fish in the region that is much greater than previously recognized. Consequently, reducing average concentrations of PCBs in fish is not likely to lead to lifting all restrictions on the consumption of Great Lakes fish. Because this measure does not clearly represent all of the contaminants that need to be addressed, it may not be useful for indicating GLRI progress toward the Action Plan's goals and objectives.

---

[40]For information on criteria for determining the extent to which an agency's performance plan provides a clear picture of intended performance, see GAO, *The Results Act: An Evaluator's Guide to Assessing Agency Performance Plans* GAO/GGD-10.1.20 (Washington, D.C.: April 1998).

[41]D. C. Evers, J . G. Wiener, C. T. Driscoll, D. A. Gay, N. Basu, B. A. Monson, K. F. Lambert, H. A. Morrison, J. T. Morgan, K. A. Williams, and A. G. Soehl, *Great Lakes Mercury Connections: The Extent and Effects of Mercury Pollution in the Great Lakes Region*, Biodiversity Research Institute, Report BRI 2011-18 (Gorham, Maine: 2011).

Monitoring practices may affect the usefulness of some measures. For example, one goal of the invasive species focus area is to eliminate the introduction of new invasive species, with a 2014 objective of reducing the yearly average rate of invasive species newly detected in the Great Lakes ecosystem by 40 percent, compared with the period from 2000 to 2009. The linked measure of progress addresses the rate at which nonnative species are newly detected in the Great Lakes ecosystem. The source of data used to evaluate this measure is a database maintained by the National Oceanic and Atmospheric Administration. According to information on this database, the identification of new species depends on the ability to find, recognize, verify, and document new species, which is, in turn, dependent on the ability to adequately sample the Great Lakes ecosystem. Officials from a state agency and four subject matter experts raised concerns about the usefulness of this measure for assessing progress toward the Action Plan objectives, noting that the number of new species detected will increase if surveillance for invasive species increases or improves. One of these experts noted that meeting the targets may not represent progress because monitoring efforts are low, and another of these experts told us that the measure needs to be combined with a known level of monitoring. Similarly, National Oceanic and Atmospheric Administration officials agreed that progress toward the targets for this measure will vary depending on the extent of monitoring and the ability of surveillance to detect new nonnative species, and they told us that, without a known level of monitoring, it may not be possible to reliably identify trends in the introduction or detection of new species using this measure. As we reported in November 2002, one attribute of successful performance measures is that they are likely to produce the same results if applied repeatedly to the same situation.[42] If efforts to identify new species depend on the ability to adequately sample the Great Lakes ecosystem and surveillance or levels of monitoring are not consistent throughout the program, then this measure may not be useful for indicating GLRI progress toward the Action Plan's goals and objectives.

Targets for some measures may not represent significant ecological improvement. EPA's Science Advisory Board reported in its 2012 review of the GLRI Action Plan that it is not clear whether the targets for the measures of progress reflect significant or measurable improvement, or

---

[42]GAO-03-143.

whether achieving the targets will result in real ecological benefit. It also noted that it is not clear how the targets were developed and, that while the measures of progress include baselines for the targets, the universe is not always defined.[43] For example, one measure in the nearshore health and nonpoint source pollution focus area addresses the amount of land with certain conservation practices implemented to reduce erosion, nutrients, and pesticides. The Action Plan reports a baseline of 165,000 acres with such practices already being implemented and identifies a 2014 target of 247,500 acres, a 50 percent increase. However, the Action Plan does not identify the universe (i.e., the total acreage of land upon which such practices could be implemented), which the Science Advisory Board reported is more than 38 million acres of agricultural land in the United States within the Great Lakes Basin. Consequently, using this universe, the 50 percent increase in acreage using such conservation measures represents a change from 0.4 percent to 0.6 percent of the total U.S. agricultural land in the Great Lakes Basin. According to the Science Advisory Board, it is not clear if this change is meaningful and how this percentage of improvement will potentially result in the restoration of the Great Lakes ecosystem. In November 2002, we reported that clarity is a key attribute of successful performance measure.[44] Without some clarification, this measure may not be useful for indicating GLRI progress toward the Action Plan's goals and objectives.

A subgroup of the Task Force agencies has been evaluating how well the measures of progress and targets are working and has identified some that will need revisions. For example, the subgroup found that some measures of progress have been difficult to implement or difficult to demonstrate scientifically, particularly in the nearshore health and nonpoint source pollution focus area. However, as this subgroup has acknowledged, there is no defined process for the Task Force agencies to revise the Action Plan, such as updating or replacing the measures of progress or for updating their targets.

---

[43]According to the Action Plan, the baseline represents the starting point for the measure, and the universe represents all that could possibly be, for example, protected, restored, or enhanced. For example, one measure in the plan is the amount of contaminated sediment remediated in the Great Lakes. The baseline is 5.5 million cubic yards of sediment, and the universe is 46 million cubic yards.

[44]GAO-03-143.

EPA and the Task Force Agencies Have Not Fully Established an Adaptive Management Plan for the GLRI

EPA and the Task Force agencies have not fully established a plan to guide an adaptive management process for the GLRI. Although there is no requirement that the Task Force establish an adaptive management plan for the GLRI, an adaptive management process could allow EPA and the Task Force agencies to evaluate whether GLRI projects are leading to the Action Plan's objectives and goals and, if needed, use the results to adjust future actions. EPA and several Task Force agencies in 2000 adopted a unified federal policy on watershed management that defined adaptive management as a type of natural resource management in which decisions are made as part of an ongoing science-based process that involves (1) testing, monitoring, and evaluating applied strategies; (2) incorporating new knowledge into management approaches that are based on scientific findings and the needs of society; and (3) using results to modify management policy, strategies, and practices.[45] This policy stated that the agencies would incorporate adaptive management principles into their programs and use adaptive management to improve watershed conditions. More recently, in the 2012 amendment to the Great Lakes Water Quality Agreement, the United States and Canada agreed to be guided by the principles and approaches of adaptive management, which is described in the agreement as a systematic process to assess the effectiveness of actions and adjust future actions to achieve the objectives of the agreement, as outcomes and ecosystem processes become better understood.

There is no universal definition for adaptive management or fixed set of steps that constitutes an adaptive management process, but key elements of this iterative process based on guidance documents from several Task Force agencies are summarized in figure 4. In addition, according to guidance from the Forest Service, adaptive management requires explicit designs that, among other things, specify documentation and monitoring protocols; roles, relationships, and responsibilities; and, assessment and evaluation processes. This guidance also notes that it is important for an adaptive management effort to have clear documentation describing details of the adaptive management process, and an absence

---

[45]U.S. Department of Agriculture, U.S. Department of Commerce, U.S. Department of Defense, U.S. Department of Energy, U.S. Department of the Interior, U.S. Environmental Protection Agency, Tennessee Valley Authority, and U.S. Army Corps of Engineers, *Unified Federal Policy for a Watershed Approach to Federal Land and Resource Management*, notice of final policy, 65 Fed. Reg. 62566 (Oct. 18, 2000).

of explicit plans can diminish the potential benefits of adaptive management.[46]

Figure 4: Key Elements of the Adaptive Management Process

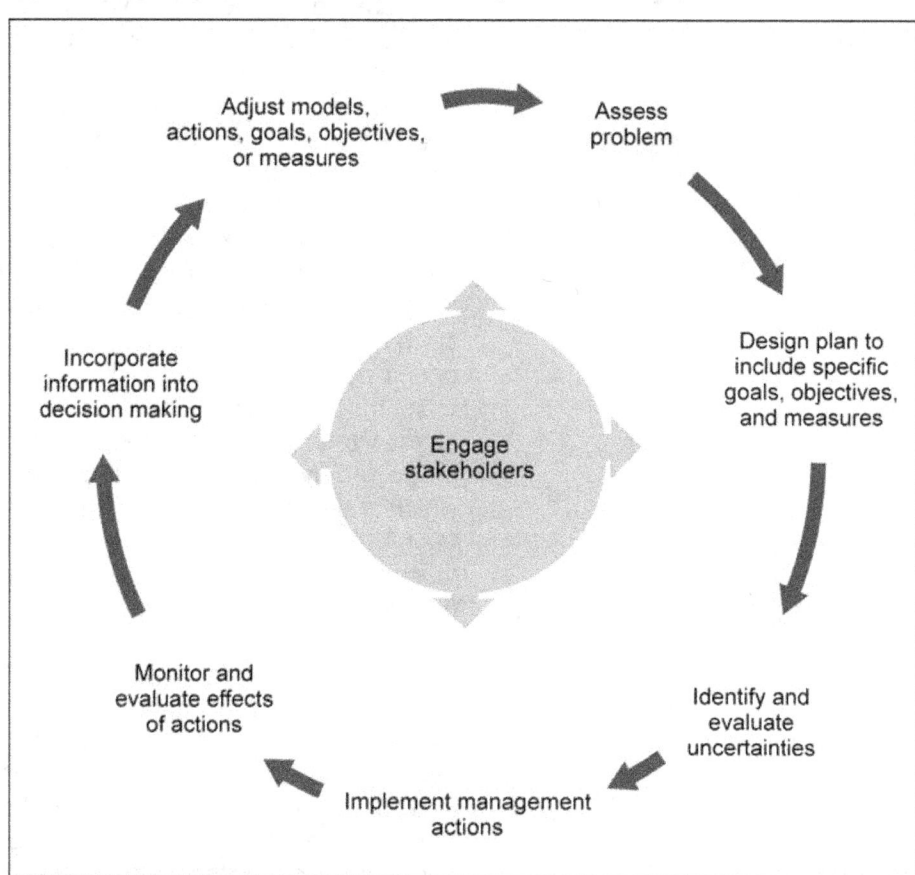

Sources: GAO analysis of guidance from the Department of the Interior,[a] U.S. Geological Survey,[b] U.S. Army Corps of Engineers,[c] Forest Service,[d] and EPA.[e]

[a]B. K. Williams and E. D. Brown, *Adaptive Management: The U.S. Department of the Interior Applications Guide*, Adaptive Management Working Group, U.S. Department of the Interior (Washington, D.C.: 2012).

---

[46]G. H. Stankey, R. N. Clark, and B. T. Bormann, *Adaptive management of natural resources: theory, concepts, and management institutions*, Gen. Tech. Rep. PNW-GTR-654: U.S. Department of Agriculture, Forest Service, Pacific Northwest Research Station (Portland, OR: 2005).

B. K. Williams, R. C. Szaro, and C. D. Shapiro, *Adaptive Management: The U.S. Department of the Interior Technical Guide*, Adaptive Management Working Group, U.S. Department of the Interior (Washington, D.C.: 2009).

[b]A. J. Atkinson, P. C. Trenham, R. N. Fisher, S. A. Hathaway, B. S. Johnson, S. G. Torres, and Y. C. Moore, *Designing Monitoring Programs In an Adaptive Management Context For Regional Multiple Species Conservation Plans*, U.S. Geological Survey Technical Report (U.S. Geological Survey Western Ecological Research Center, Sacramento, CA: 2004).

[c]RECOVER 2010, *Comprehensive Everglades Restoration Plan Adaptive Management Integration Guide*, Restoration Coordination and Verification (Jacksonville, FL and West Palm Beach, FL: U.S. Army Corps of Engineers, Jacksonville District and South Florida Water Management District, 2010).

[d]G. H. Stankey, R. N. Clark, and B. T. Bormann, *Adaptive Management of Natural Resources: Theory, Concepts, and Management Institutions*, Gen. Tech. Rep. PNW-GTR-654 (Portland, OR: U.S. Department of Agriculture, Forest Service, Pacific Northwest Research Station, 2005).

[e]EPA, *Watershed Analysis and Management (WAM) Guide for States and Communities: EPA Watershed Analysis and Management Project* (Washington, D.C.: 2003), and EPA, Handbook for Developing Watershed Plans to Restore and Protect Our Waters, EPA 841-B-08-002 (Washington, D.C.: 2008).

In its 2012 review of the Action Plan, EPA's Science Advisory Board found that the GLRI Action Plan did not establish an adaptive management framework and recommended that EPA develop a science-based plan that, when coupled with the Action Plan, would create an adaptive management framework for the GLRI. In response to this recommendation, in May 2013, the Task Force agencies released the draft *GLRI Adaptive Science-Based Framework for Great Lakes Restoration*, or draft framework, for public comment.[47]

The draft framework recommends use of an "adaptive restoration" approach for the GLRI that includes most of the key elements of adaptive management. According to the draft framework, adaptive restoration involves exploring alternative ways to meet the goals and objectives in the Action Plan, predicting the outcomes of alternatives based on the current state of knowledge, implementing one or more of these alternatives, monitoring to learn about the impacts of restoration actions, and incorporating new knowledge into restoration strategies that are based on scientific findings and the needs of society. However, the draft framework does not provide details on how the elements of adaptive management will be implemented. For example, neither the draft framework, nor the Action Plan, addresses how the agencies will complete the adaptive management loop by incorporating the information gained in future decision making and adjusting the GLRI, if needed. The

---

[47]Science Subgroup of the Great Lakes Regional Working Group, *Great Lakes Restoration Initiative Adaptive Science-Based Framework for Great Lakes Restoration* (May 21, 2013).

draft framework indicates that re-assessment of the Action Plan goals, objectives, and measures of progress should be considered every 5 years. However, neither the framework nor the Action Plan outlines a process for assessing or incorporating new information or altering the Action Plan, such as by refining the measures or their targets, as recommended by the adaptive management section of EPA's 2003 guidance for states and communities on watershed analysis and management.[48] For example, neither the draft framework nor the Action Plan identifies decision thresholds or criteria for making changes, which the Science Advisory Board's 2012 report and EPA's 2003 guidance have identified as important.

In addition, the draft framework does not include two of the key elements of adaptive management shown in figure 4: engaging stakeholders, and identifying and evaluating uncertainties.

Engaging stakeholders. According to guidance from several Task Force agencies, active and sustained stakeholder involvement is essential for effective implementation of adaptive management.[49] The draft framework does not explicitly include stakeholder engagement as an element of the adaptive restoration process. It acknowledges that engaging scientists, stakeholders, and the general public should be considered for updating the GLRI over time and states that interactive engagement in setting goals and objectives is a key element for producing results. Nevertheless, it does not address how the Task Force agencies will ensure ongoing stakeholder engagement in the GLRI. Without explicit plans in the draft framework for engaging stakeholders, it is not clear how the Task Force agencies will consider and account for potential changes in stakeholder perspectives and priorities. As the Department of the Interior's guidance notes, conflicting priorities among stakeholders can be enough to prevent the successful implementation of adaptive management.[50] This guidance also explains that differing stakeholder views about how natural processes work and how they respond to management are examples of uncertainties that can limit the effectiveness of management efforts.

[48]EPA, *Watershed Analysis and Management (WAM) Guide for States and Communities.*

[49]For example, see Williams and Brown, *Adaptive Management;* Stankey et al., *Adaptive Management of Natural Resources;* and RECOVER 2010, *Comprehensive Everglades Restoration Plan Adaptive Management Integration Guide.*

[50]Williams and Brown, *Adaptive Management.*

Identifying and evaluating uncertainties. Neither the draft framework, nor the Action Plan, identifies, prioritizes, and evaluates critical scientific or policy uncertainties. In addition, the draft framework does not include such uncertainties in its list of elements of adaptive restoration planning. Such uncertainties could include critical assumptions, gaps in knowledge, or uncertainties about the relationships between ecological processes and stresses, such as the potential effects of climate change on the Great Lakes. Identifying and explicitly accounting for critical uncertainties in designing the GLRI could increase the likelihood that the GLRI will meet its goals and objectives. Several Task Force agencies have emphasized the use of models as an important way to evaluate and account for such uncertainties by, for example, representing how the ecosystem may respond to restoration actions or environmental changes.[51] The draft framework notes that predictive modeling plays an important role in adaptive restoration, and it recommends evaluation of uncertainties in the context of reporting on progress.[52] However, the framework does not identify and account for critical uncertainties.

Task Force Agencies and Nonfederal Stakeholders Report GLRI Progress, but Overall Great Lakes Restoration Progress Is Difficult to Quantify

The Task Force agencies have issued two GLRI progress reports, but the reports include few specific examples of progress. To obtain further insights about GLRI progress, we surveyed nonfederal GLRI stakeholders and interviewed Task Force agency officials. However, quantifying overall Great Lakes restoration progress is difficult for several reasons, including the unique environmental conditions of each of the Great Lakes.

---

[51]Williams and Brown, *Adaptive Management*. Williams et al., *Adaptive Management*. Atkinson et al., *Designing Monitoring Programs*. RECOVER 2010, *Comprehensive Everglades Restoration Plan Adaptive Management Integration Guide*. Stankey et al., *Adaptive Management of Natural Resources*.

[52]For example, it states that progress reports should (1) attempt to consider the influence of potentially confounding developments such as natural environmental variation, along with regional and global trends such as climate change, shifts in human population numbers, and changing patterns of land use and (2) include relevant evaluations of the uncertainty and assumptions associated with particular restoration actions and long-term sustainability of ecosystem health.

As we noted previously, the Task Force agencies have issued two GLRI progress reports to Congress; one on fiscal year 2011 progress and one on progress in fiscal year 2010. EPA officials told us that the report on progress in fiscal year 2011 includes more information and was released earlier than the fiscal year 2010 report because GLRI funding was available late in fiscal year 2010 and not as much was achieved that year. Both reports identified whether the targets for the GLRI Action Plan's 28 measures of progress had been met or exceeded in the related fiscal year, or that data were unavailable for a specific measure. For example, the fiscal year 2011 report states that 15 measures were met or exceeded, 9 measures were not met, and data were not available to determine the status of 4 measures. However, as we noted earlier, the measures may not provide sufficiently comprehensive or useful information for a number of reasons, including that the measures do not capture the results of many of the GLRI projects and that some measures or their targets may not be indicative of progress.

The fiscal year 2011 report also includes broad statements about whether the GLRI is achieving goals, objectives, and measures of progress that are followed by several examples of results and highlights of progress made or expected in two projects in each of the five Action Plan focus areas.[53] For example, in the invasive species focus area, the report states that:

In the first years of the GLRI, no new aquatic invasive species populations have been detected in the Great Lakes. The GLRI is at the forefront of invasive species prevention, control, and rapid response. The GLRI is supporting investments in technologies that prevent the introduction of invasive species, including the Department of Transportation's Maritime Administration's verification of new ballast water treatment technologies, which is an important step before conducting ship-scale testing.

However, except for the two projects highlighted in each focus area, the fiscal year 2011 report does not identify the GLRI projects that led to the progress achieved. In addition, neither of the two reports integrates accomplishment and progress information into conclusions about overall GLRI progress or contains specific information about the extent of progress toward GLRI goals, and neither includes an assessment of changes in the health of the Great Lakes ecosystem that could be

---

[53]The fiscal year 2010 report includes a list of five to nine projects in each of the Action Plan focus areas, some of which include a description of progress made.

attributed to the projects. As a result, the information in the GLRI progress reports was not sufficient for determining if GLRI projects had led to the described progress and how much progress has been made in restoring the health of the Great Lakes ecosystem.

Nonfederal Stakeholder and Task Force Agency Examples of GLRI Progress

In light of the limited information included in the two GLRI progress reports, we sought to obtain further insights by surveying nonfederal stakeholders and interviewing officials from Task Force agencies. The information we gathered in the survey allows us to provide more information on how nonfederal stakeholders describe GLRI progress, and it is not intended to determine the extent of GLRI progress toward restoring the health of the Great Lakes ecosystem. When asked to provide examples of how one or more of their organization's GLRI projects had benefitted the Great Lakes ecosystem, 87 percent (153) of the 176 respondents provided at least one example of how one or more of their GLRI projects had benefited, or was expected to benefit, the Great Lakes ecosystem in each of the five focus areas. Specifically:

- 55 percent (96) of respondents provided at least one example of how one or more of their GLRI projects had directly benefited the Great Lakes ecosystem, such as by restoring habitat or by trapping invasive species.

- 27 percent (47) of respondents provided at least one example of how one or more of their GLRI projects indirectly benefited the Great Lakes ecosystem, such as by improving the understanding of part of the ecosystem or identifying future restoration work.[54]

- 44 percent (77) of respondents reported that they expected at least one of their projects to result in a direct or indirect benefit to the ecosystem, but that it was too early to report a benefit at this time.

- 13 percent (23) of respondents did not provide an example of how one of their projects had, or was expected to, benefit the Great Lakes ecosystem.

---

[54]Because some respondents provided examples of more than one type of benefit, the sum of the percent of respondents that provided examples exceeds the 87 percent response rate.

A majority of the survey respondents and Task Force agency officials we interviewed reported progress toward the overall GLRI goal of restoring the health of the Great Lakes ecosystem. The following examples represent a broad range of GLRI progress in each of the five focus areas as reported by survey respondents, through the survey and follow-up interviews, and by Task Force agency officials, in interviews, and do not represent the only types of GLRI projects being implemented:

Toxic substances and areas of concern

- One survey respondent reported that her organization received two GLRI grants to help clean up the Presque Isle Bay area of concern in Lake Erie, in Pennsylvania; the two grants totaled $664,789. The respondent told us that, prior to the GLRI, the organization was devoting all of its resources to addressing only one of the specific conditions—fish tumors—that were responsible for the bay being identified as an area of concern, and that GLRI funding made it possible for her organization to do additional work. Specifically, GLRI funding enabled the organization to undertake a number of monitoring and investigative projects; develop a target for being removed from the list of areas of concern; and, develop a long-term monitoring, restoration, and protection plan for the bay's watershed. The respondent reported that GLRI funding was also used for specific investigations in the watershed that will provide her organization with an updated set of data to use in identifying priority areas for restoration and protection. According to the respondent, without that information, the organization would not have a blueprint to maintain and continue protecting the bay. In December 2012, 21 years after the bay had been identified as an area of concern, the survey respondent told us in an interview that her organization was in the process of sending a formal request to remove Presque Isle Bay's designation as an area of concern. EPA announced in February 2013 that the bay had been delisted. It is the second U.S. area of concern to be removed from the list. The respondent estimated that GLRI funding had accelerated the process of removing Presque Isle Bay from the list of areas of concern by 10 years.

- Officials we interviewed from the U.S. Geological Survey told us that the agency had used GLRI funds to complete three basin-wide sampling efforts of the water column, bottom sediments, and two other types of samples across the entire Great Lakes Basin as a part of its methylmercury sampling and analysis project. Methylmercury— an organic form of mercury—is a highly toxic substance that can build up in predatory fish, including fish that people eat. According to the officials, the sampling efforts took place in August 2010, April 2011, and August 2011, and data from these efforts have revealed a previously unknown source of methylmercury that likely is the dominant source leading to elevated concentrations in fish throughout the Great Lakes.

Figure 5: A Depiction of the Mercury Cycle

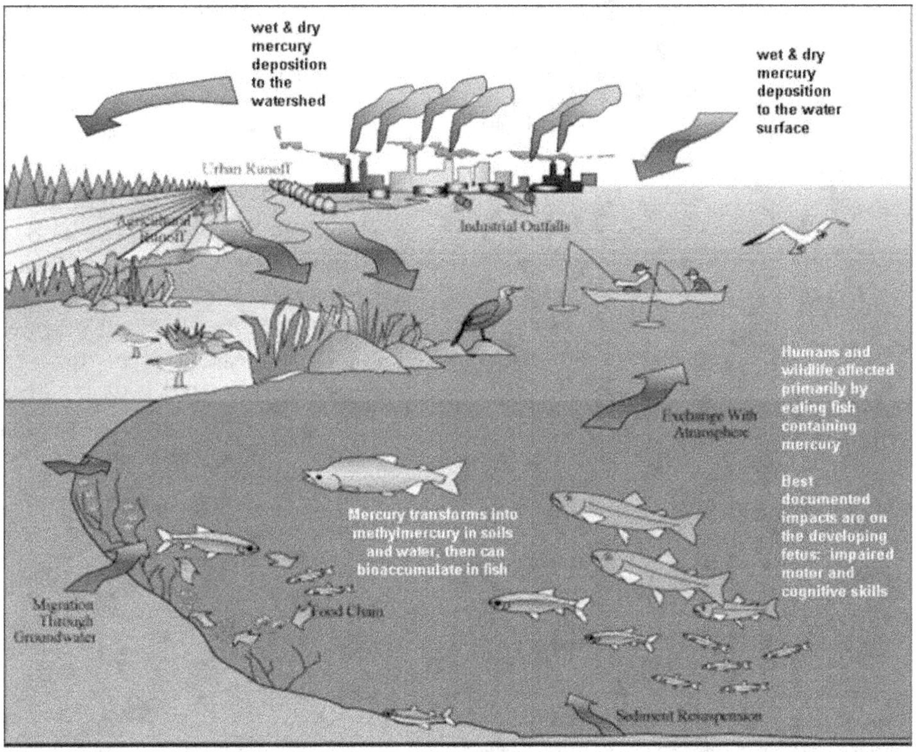

Source: National Oceanic and Atmospheric Administration.

Mercury

Mercury is a highly toxic metal that can pose health risks to wildlife and people. Specifically, high levels of mercury exposure can harm the brain, heart, kidneys, lungs, and immune system of people of all ages. People are most commonly exposed to an organic form of mercury called methylmercury. Methylmercury accumulates up the food chain, so big fish that eat smaller fish tend to contain more methylmercury. People are primarily exposed to methylmercury through eating contaminated fish. According to a 2011 Biodiversity Research Institute report, mercury pollution is ubiquitous across the Great Lakes region, primarily as a result of emissions from coal-fired power plants, and five states in the region have issued statewide consumption advisories for mercury in fish from all freshwaters, two have issued statewide advisories for mercury in fish from all lakes, and one has issued advisories for specific water bodies.

Notes: D.C. Evers, J.G. Wiener, C.T. Driscoll, D.A. Gay, N. Basu, B.A. Monson, K.F. Lambert, H.A. Morrison, J.T. Morgan, K.A. Williams, A.G. Soehl, 2011, *Great Lakes Mercury Connections: The Extent and Effects of Mercury Pollution in the Great Lakes Region* (Gorham, Maine: Biodiversity Research Institute, 2011).

Invasive species

- One survey respondent reported progress made by a project to improve control of sea lampreys, an invasive species in the Great Lakes, for which his organization had received $8,203,561 in GLRI funding. According to the U.S. Geological Survey, sea lampreys have devastated fish communities in the Great Lakes by feeding on the bodily fluids of host fish, such as the native lake trout. According to the respondent, the project worked to develop a new sea lamprey control technique that relies on the sea lamprey's sense of smell. The respondent reported that field trials using this technique increased trapping efficiencies by up to 53 percent and that traps used with this technique can capture more than twice as many sea lampreys as traps that do not use the technique. According to the respondent, this

GAO-13-797 Great Lakes Restoration Initiative

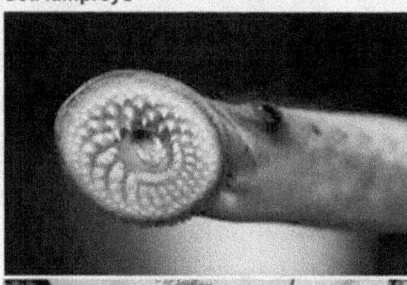

Sea lampreys

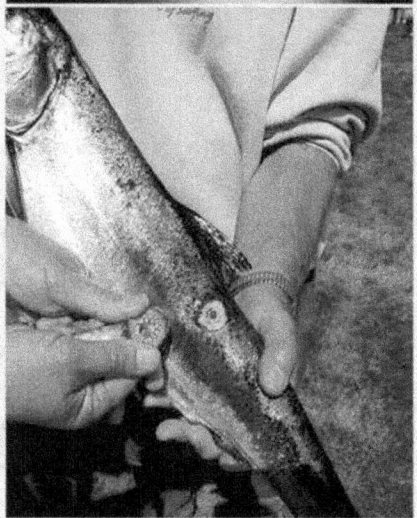

Source: Great Lakes Fishery Commission.

Sea lampreys are parasites that attach to fish and feed on the fish's body fluids, often killing the fish. A single lamprey can kill up to about 40 pounds of fish in its lifetime. Sea lampreys prey on all species of Great Lakes fish, including economically important fish such as lake trout, salmon, whitefish, chubs, and walleye. Sea lampreys were a major cause of the collapse of lake trout, whitefish, and chub populations in the Great Lakes during the 1940s and 1950s. Sea lampreys are native to the Atlantic Ocean. They were observed in Lake Erie in 1921 following improvements to the canal that bypasses Niagara Falls and were observed in all five of the Great Lakes by 1939.

new technique may make it possible not only to capture more sea lampreys but also to reduce the amount of pesticides introduced into the Great Lakes that are used to kill sea lampreys.

- Officials we interviewed from the U.S. Coast Guard told us that the agency's invasive species-related projects will increase its enforcement capability and address some technical problems relating to the installation and operation of freshwater ballast treatment systems for vessels operating on the Great Lakes. Ballast water is water that is taken into or discharged from a ship to accommodate changes in weight as a ship loads or unloads cargo. According to the U.S. Coast Guard, ballast treatment systems are intended to reduce the number of invasive species that can be transported into the Great Lakes in ballast water. The U.S. Coast Guard's Research and Development Center worked with the Naval Research Laboratory to design, build, test, and verify a system for testing treated ballast water under both shoreside and shipboard conditions. According to U.S. Coast Guard officials, this project will facilitate rigorous testing of the performance of ballast water treatment systems under shipboard conditions, ensuring greater protection against the introduction of invasive species into the Great Lakes.

Nearshore health and nonpoint source pollution

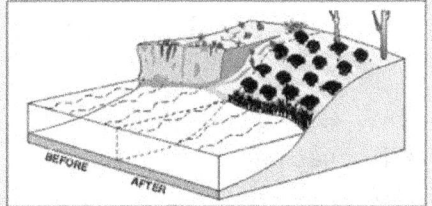

Buffer zones and filter strips

Source: Natural Resources Conservation Service.

Buffer zones and filter strips are conservation practices that farms can use to reduce erosion and nutrient risks. They are strips of natural vegetation along the banks of a stream, lake, or other water body that separate the water from developed areas. Buffers are important because they

- provide natural habitat for birds, mammals, and other wildlife;

- provide shade to keep stream water cooler, which can improve habitat for instream organisms such as fish and frogs;

- stabilize stream banks with their root systems and prevent erosion; and

- preserve water quality by capturing sediment and chemicals from runoff, and slow runoff to help prevent flooding.

- One survey respondent reported that her organization received $85,000 in GLRI funding for a project to reduce the amount of bacteria in beach sand at a park on Lake Erie, in New York. According to the respondent, work completed in 2011 with GLRI funds determined that beach sand is acting as a reservoir for *Escherichia coli*, abbreviated as *E. coli*, which can negatively impact public health.[55] The organization then compared three sand grooming techniques to no beach grooming. According to the respondent, the results indicated that sand grooming using a specific tractor attachment can reduce the amount of bacteria in the sand. In 2012, the organization compared water quality when sand was groomed using two different grooming techniques. The respondent reported that preliminary results indicate that grooming the beach daily with the specific tractor attachment significantly reduced the number of beach closures. The respondent reported that this fiscal year 2011 to 2012 GLRI project resulted in an improvement in water quality.

- The Natural Resources Conservation Service received $75 million in GLRI funding from fiscal years 2010 to 2012 to target conservation efforts in selected priority areas. According to an agency official, this funding provides an opportunity to implement additional scientifically proven conservation practices in the priority watersheds, accelerating conservation practice implementation above what other programs would have provided. Landowners can take advantage of GLRI funds through a Natural Resources Conservation Service cost-share assistance program to install conservation practices. The agency helps landowners with conservation planning using various conservation practices, such as cover crops, conservation crop rotations, filter strips, prescribed grazing, and wetlands restoration. For example, the practice of cover crops establishes close-growing grasses, or other crops, to help improve soil and water quality by reducing soil erosion, among other things. A filter strip is a strip of herbaceous vegetation that is situated between crop or grazing land and a stream, river, or wetland, in order to reduce contaminated runoff. An agency official reported that GLRI funded efforts have led to the use of cover crops and filter strips on nearly 70,000 acres and 143 acres of priority watersheds respectively. For example, one landowner

---

[55]*E. coli* are a large and diverse group of bacteria found in the environment, foods, and intestines of people and animals. Some strains can cause pneumonia and other illnesses in humans who may come into contact with *E. coli* in rivers and lakes contaminated by human or animal feces.

used the funds to develop a prescribed grazing system that encourages groundwater recharge, improves soil quality and prevents sediment and nutrient losses. The landowner is also installing a waste collection system to keep contaminated water out of nearby surface water and plans to plant 34 acres of cover crop.

Habitat and wildlife protection and restoration

Barriers to fish passage
Before

After

Source: Ducks Unlimited.

Barriers to fish passage, such as dams and misaligned culverts, result in habitat fragmentation and can impede the passage of fish species to and from their historic spawning grounds. According to a 2010 report by the Association of Fish and Wildlife Agencies, one-third of all Great Lakes fish are estimated to use tributaries as their principal spawning and nursery habitats and, in the Lake Michigan watershed alone, barriers to fish passage have reduced nearly 19,000 miles of available stream habitat to 3,300 miles. Reconnecting fragmented streams and rivers increases habitat connectivity and can create healthier aquatic ecosystems for fish.

Note: National Fish Habitat Board, *Through a Fish's Eye: The Status of Fish Habitats in the United States 2010* (Washington, D.C.: Association of Fish and Wildlife Agencies, 2010). 20.

- A survey respondent reported that his organization had a project to help restore a marsh area that is among the roughly 15 costal marsh areas along Lake Michigan's Lower Peninsula shoreline. The organization received $783,823 in GLRI funds for the project. One component of the project was to replace seven misaligned culverts. According to the respondent, the new culverts will allow unimpeded fish passage to more than 12 miles of stream habitat, which improves habitat for trout and other aquatic organisms. In addition, the respondent reported that the project restored a mile-long section of trout stream back to its original watercourse. This was necessary because the hydrology of an adjacent 75-acre wetland had been significantly degraded when the trout stream had been diverted into a straightened channel decades ago. The project also resulted in the eradication of types of invasive plants. The survey respondent reported that this project will improve fisheries habitat, help restore hydrology to a large wetland for waterfowl and many other species of wildlife and fish, and improve public recreational opportunities.

- Officials from the Fish and Wildlife Service told us that the agency has received $11,590,857 in GLRI funds in fiscal years 2010 to 2012 for a project that focuses on restoring habitats for native lake sturgeon, brook trout, migratory birds, and threatened and endangered species populations within the Great Lakes Basin by removing barriers to fish passage, stabilizing stream banks and riparian areas (narrow vegetated areas adjoining rivers, streams, and lakes), improving in-stream habitat and restoring costal, wetland and upland areas. According to agency officials, the project has protected, restored, or enhanced more than 2,000 acres of wetlands and uplands, removed or bypassed more than 30 fish passage barriers, and reopened more than 210 stream miles to fish movement. Agency officials said that improving aquatic connectivity in the Great Lakes Basin is one of the more prominent achievements of the project, and that removing barriers to fish passage creates a healthier aquatic habitat and improves water quality and sediment management. In addition, according to agency officials, free-flowing rivers provide new recreational opportunities.

GAO-13-797 Great Lakes Restoration Initiative

Accountability, education, monitoring, evaluation, communication, and partnerships

- One survey respondent reported that his organization received GLRI funding to map and describe all of the wastewater treatment plants in the Great Lakes Basin, both in the United States and Canada, and to develop a binational aquatic invasive species response plan. The respondent's organization received $300,000 in GLRI funding for these projects. According to the respondent, the project to map and describe wastewater treatment plants resulted in the first ever binational map of these facilities and will inform management decisions about the level and consistency of water treatment and help protect human and environmental health. In addition, the respondent reported that the aquatic invasive species response plan developed by his organization provides a foundation for work on a basinwide plan that will be an important backup plan in the event that aquatic invasive species prevention efforts fail. According to the respondent, the plan his organization developed will directly assist the governments of the United States and Canada in meeting their obligations under the 2012 amendment to the Great Lakes Water Quality Agreement, which requires the two governments to develop and implement an early detection and rapid response initiative for aquatic invasive species, among other things.

- Officials we interviewed from the National Oceanic and Atmospheric Administration told us that the agency's dissemination of training materials for educators and climate curricula for elementary through high school students, which is customized for the Great Lakes region, is on target to reach more than 3,000 students and 50 teachers by the end of fiscal year 2013. As a result, officials said, the number of institutions incorporating this information into existing curricula far exceeds the GLRI Action Plan targets. Specifically, the Action Plan's 2013 target for the measure that addresses the number of educational institutions incorporating Great Lakes protection and stewardship criteria into their environmental education curricula is 10 institutions. This measure corresponds to the Action Plan's goal to increase outreach and education for the Great Lakes so that students understand the benefits and ecosystem functions of the Great Lakes and are able to make decisions to ensure that restoration investments are enhanced over time.

In addition to these examples of progress, respondents to our survey and other stakeholders we interviewed reported that the GLRI had allowed them to do restoration work that they previously identified as important but could not undertake because of limited funds or staff, among other reasons. For example, one survey respondent noted that due to GLRI funding, progress has been made on problems that had been languishing for years due to inadequate funding such as high-priority restoration projects, aquatic invasive species control, and actions to reduce beneficial use impairments. In addition, a state agency official we interviewed told us that without GLRI funding his state would not have had the capacity to help coordinate restoration efforts for areas of concern or conduct necessary monitoring of fish toxicity. Furthermore, in commenting on a draft of this report, National Park Service officials noted that GLRI funds have proven to be invaluable for helping the Service accomplish significant restoration of wetlands and areas affected by invasive species, among other things.

Overall Great Lakes Restoration Progress Is Difficult to Quantify

We, and other organizations, have documented the difficulties associated with efforts to quantify overall progress toward Great Lakes restoration. For example, we reported in 2004 that it is difficult to describe restoration progress across the basin because of the unique environmental conditions of each of the Great Lakes.[56] Specifically, the Great Lakes are not one contiguous water body but rather distinct lakes with unique environmental conditions—such as lake depth—that present challenges to setting goals and developing a monitoring system that can be used to describe restoration progress across the basin and also capture the uniqueness of each lake. In addition, according to a 2006 United Nations report, it is usually difficult, and sometimes impossible, to attribute changes in the state of a large ecosystem solely to the efforts of a specific ecosystem management program. [57] Furthermore, several Task Force agency officials, nonfederal stakeholders, and subject matter experts told us that it may take time for some Great Lakes restoration efforts to show measurable results.

EPA officials told us that it may not be possible to summarize Great Lakes restoration progress with one simple statement due to the size and complexity of the Great Lakes ecosystem. They said that when the Action Plan was created, the Task Force agencies incorporated a measure the agency had created as part of its GPRA reporting requirements, the Great Lakes 40-point scale (also called the Great Lakes Index), as a measure of

---

[56]GAO-04-1024.

[57]United Nations Environmental Program and Global Programme of Action for the Protection of the Marine Environment from Land-based Activities, *Ecosystem-based Management: Markers for Assessing Progress* (The Hague, Netherlands: 2006).

progress intended to represent progress across the focus areas by measuring improvement in the overall health of the aquatic ecosystem. The index rates eight indicators on a scale from 1 to 5, where 1 is poor, and 5 is good, to produce an assessment of overall Great Lakes health that is represented by one number.[58]

However, some stakeholders and subject matter experts we interviewed raised concerns about the index and some of its indicators. For example, they said that the index is missing key ecosystem indicators, such as those related to invasive species and the health of native species. In addition, they said that the index is better suited for assessments of long-term, as opposed to annual, changes in the health of the ecosystem. EPA officials also questioned how meaningful it was to use just one number to convey information about the state of the multiple ecosystems and indicators within the Great Lake basin.

EPA officials also explained that the GLRI is a relatively new undertaking and that getting visible, lake-wide and basin-wide ecosystem improvements from Great Lakes restoration efforts is a slow process. According to the officials, benefits, such as improvements in areas of concern, are being seen at the local level and by the end of the GLRI's lifespan in 2014, EPA will be able to show progress at a local level as a step toward improving the health of the lakes overall.

The Task Force agencies' draft framework includes direction to report on restoration progress and accomplishments, and transfer knowledge and lessons learned, among other things. The draft framework also notes that, while assembling project specific results can begin to offer a picture of cumulative progress and local success, reporting on GLRI at the program level can inform whether or not the GLRI is making restoration progress at other levels, such as the regional, lake, or ecosystem level.

---

[58]The eight indicators are coastal wetlands, phosphorus concentrations, area of concern sediment contamination, benthic health, fish tissue contamination, beach closures, drinking water quality, and air toxics deposition. The ratings for each indicator are added together to create the index score. Improvements in the index would indicate that fewer toxics are entering the food chain; ecosystem and human health is better protected; fish are safer to eat; water is safer to drink; and beaches are safer for swimming.

Nonfederal Stakeholders Identified Key Factors That May Affect and May Limit GLRI Progress

In response to our survey, respondents reported on what they believed to be the key factors that may affect and may limit GLRI progress. They cited practical issues related to implementing GLRI projects, such as the time it takes to complete quality assurance requirements and obtain permits. They also cited broader issues outside the scope of the Action Plan, for which realistic solutions may be expensive, pointing in particular to inadequate infrastructure for wastewater and stormwater and the effects of climate change.

Factors Related to Implementing GLRI Projects Affected Progress

Survey respondents most often reported that their GLRI projects started later than planned because of quality assurance requirements and the length of time needed to obtain permits. It is important to emphasize that quality assurance requirements for environmental programs play a critical role in ensuring the success of those programs and that permits for environmental activities are required by a number of federal and state laws. Moreover, survey respondents did not suggest that either process should be eliminated when asked to comment on GLRI's quality assurance requirements. Nonetheless, later start times can slow GLRI implementation and, as a result, may affect the pace of progress.

- *Quality assurance requirements.* Organizations that receive GLRI funds through federal grants may be required to meet specific quality assurance requirements for projects and tasks involving environmental data in order to receive the funds.[59] Seventy-seven percent (135) of the 176 survey respondents reported that they needed to complete quality assurance requirements for at least one of their GLRI projects and, that on average, it took nearly 4 months to complete those requirements. Of those 135 respondents, 28 percent (38) reported that their projects started later than planned because of the time it took to complete quality assurance requirements, and 13 percent (17) reported that they could not start their project until the next spring because the ground or water was frozen. EPA officials told us that the GLRI quality assurance process was slow at the start of

---

[59]According to the EPA, the success of an environmental project depends on the quality of the environmental data collected and used in decision making. As part of the process of ensuring that projects have quality data, a grantee creates a document that is intended to serve as a tool for project managers and planners to document the type and quality of data needed for environmental decisions and to describe the methods for collecting and assessing those data. There are neither time limits associated with this process for the GLRI, nor is there a generally accepted length of time for completing these requirements.

the program because the agency had not previously assessed quality assurance requirements for the kind of work being proposed in some of the projects. However, several survey respondents reported that the time it takes to complete GLRI quality assurance requirements has decreased since the program began in fiscal year 2010.

- *Time needed to obtain permits.* Organizations implementing GLRI projects might need to obtain federal or state permits for certain efforts, such as using herbicides to reduce invasive species, conducting controlled burning to enrich soil nutrients, or enhancing habitat for endangered species and communities. About half (87) of the 176 survey respondents reported that they needed a permit for at least one of their GLRI projects and that it took an average of 5 months to obtain the necessary permits. Of those 87 respondents, 31 reported that their projects started later than planned as a result of the time needed to obtain permits, and 13 reported that they could not start their project until the next spring because the ground or water was frozen. In addition, in the fiscal year 2011 GLRI progress report, the Task Force agencies identified permit processing as one of the factors for slowed project implementation for the habitat and wildlife protection and restoration measure of progress addressing the number of acres of coastal, upland, and island habitats protected, restored, and enhanced.

Survey respondents also reported that the timing of award notification resulted in later-than-planned start times for their GLRI projects (30 percent, or 52 out of 176, respondents),[60] and that weather events limited the implementation of their GLRI projects (26 percent, or 45 out of 176, respondents). Specifically, 16 percent (29) reported that weather events caused their GLRI projects to be completed later than planned, 15 percent (27) reported weather events caused a suspension of GLRI activities, and 6 percent (11) reported that weather events resulted in later-than-planned start times for their GLRI projects.[61] Weather events may cause GLRI projects to start later than planned because work cannot proceed on some projects—such as those that involve planting, doing construction, or monitoring stormwater—if there is a drought, too much

---

[60] The timing of award notification is the timing of when an organization received notice that its GLRI project would be funded.

[61] Because some respondents reported that weather events affected their GLRI projects in more than one way, the sum of the percent of respondents that reported specific effects of weather events exceeds the 26 percent response rate.

rain, or the ground does not freeze in winter, among other things. For example, three survey respondents reported that work on their projects in wetlands was delayed because the wetlands involved with their organization's projects did not sufficiently freeze one winter.

Factors Outside the Scope of the Action Plan May Limit GLRI Progress

Once started, the success of GLRI projects and of the GLRI as a whole can depend upon factors outside the scope of the Action Plan—that is, factors that are not addressed by the Action Plan's long-term goals, objectives, or measures of progress—that affect the Great Lakes ecosystem. One such factor is atmospheric deposition, which is a process that transfers pollutants from the air to the earth's surface and can significantly impair water quality in the nation's rivers, lakes, bays, and estuaries, and harm human health and aquatic ecosystems.[62] Airborne pollutants transferred by atmospheric deposition can fall to the ground in precipitation or as a gas or particle and be deposited either directly onto the surface of a water body or onto land and then transported into a water body through runoff. Atmospheric deposition contributed to the presence of toxaphene in the Great Lakes. Toxaphene is an insecticide that was once primarily used in southern states from 1947 to 1980, and it was banned in the United States for all uses in 1990. It is toxic for many aquatic organisms and accumulates in fish and shellfish causing health problems in humans who consume them.

We asked survey respondents to rank nine factors that are not addressed in the Action Plan on the basis of their potential to limit the restoration of the health of the Great Lakes ecosystem. As indicated in figure 5, survey respondents most frequently reported that inadequate infrastructure for wastewater or stormwater (72 percent, or 126 of 176, respondents) and the effects of climate change (65 percent, or 114 of 176, respondents) have the greatest potential to limit the restoration of the health of the Great Lakes' ecosystem in comparison with other factors outside the scope of the Action Plan. Survey respondents also reported that factors such as the removal of water from the Great Lakes for use outside of the region and the effects of population growth in the Great Lakes region have the potential to limit the restoration of the health of the Great Lakes'

---

[62]For information on atmospheric deposition, see GAO, *Water Quality: EPA Faces Challenges in Addressing Damage Caused by Airborne Pollutants,* GAO-13-39 (Washington, D.C.: Jan. 24, 2013).

ecosystem to a great or very great extent by 57 percent (101 out of 176 respondents) and 49 percent (87 out of 176 respondents) respectively.

Figure □: □urve□ Res□on□ents Rate□ □a□tors O□tsi□e t□e □□o□e o□t□e Great Lakes Restoration Initiative A□tion P□an □□at □ave t□e Potentia□ to Li□it t□e Restoration o□ t□e □ea□t□ o□t□e Great Lakes □□os□ste□ to a Great or □er□ Great □□tent

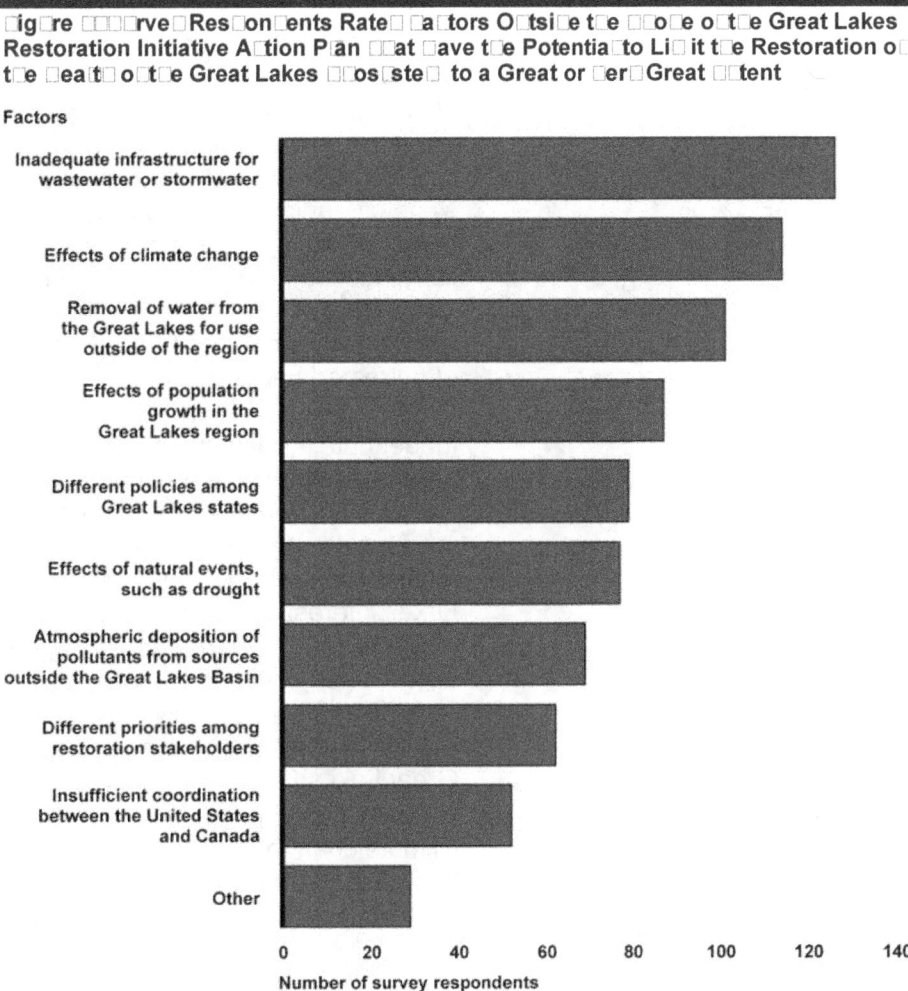

Source: GAO analysis of survey responses.

In addition, we asked 21 Great Lakes subject matter experts we interviewed to rank these factors, and 13 of the 21 experts identified the same top two factors the survey respondents did, noting that both inadequate infrastructure for wastewater or stormwater and the effects of climate change have the potential to limit the restoration of the health of the Great Lakes ecosystem to a great or very great extent.

GAO-13-797 Great Lakes Restoration Initiative

| Infrastructure | Inadequate infrastructure for wastewater or stormwater refers to the deteriorating condition of the nation's wastewater systems. These systems include sewer pipes that convey wastewater from homes and businesses to treatment facilities before discharging it into water bodies or land. In a 2004 report to Congress, EPA estimated that more than 1.2 million miles of pipes delivered wastewater into these systems. EPA has also reported that the vast majority of the pipes making up the nation's wastewater systems were installed more than 50 years ago and are reaching the end of their useful lives. In addition to the age of these systems, their conveyance capacity (i.e., the rate at which they can transport water) is often exceeded during rainfall or snowmelt, which adds to the discharge of wastewater into U.S. surface waters. According to the American Society of Civil Engineers, the age and inadequate capacity of wastewater infrastructure systems lead to the discharge billion of gallons of untreated wastewater into U.S. surface waters each year.[63] |

Inadequate infrastructure can cause conditions that may slow, if not negate, restoration efforts, such as to improve water quality or reduce the number of days a beach is closed. This is because most wastewater systems are designed to discharge flows that exceed conveyance capacity directly to rivers, streams, and other surface waters. One Great Lakes interest group reported that five U.S. cities alone discharged 41 billion gallons of untreated sewage and stormwater into the Great Lakes from January 2009 to January 2010.[64] In its most recent clean water needs survey report, EPA stated that $19.7 billion was needed to address publicly owned wastewater and stormwater infrastructure needs in the Great Lakes Basin.[65]

Climate Change

Climate change is associated with increasing land and water temperatures and rising sea levels. There is uncertainty about the precise future effects of climate change on any particular region of the country,

---

[63]The American Society of Civil Engineers represents more than 140,000 members of the civil engineering profession worldwide.

[64]Healing Our Waters – Great Lakes Coalition, *Turning the Tide: Investing in Wastewater Infrastructure to Create Jobs and Solve the Sewage Crisis in the Great Lakes* (Ann Arbor, MI: August 2010). According to the report, data for this statement was provided by the five cities and EPA.

[65]EPA, *Clean Watershed Needs Survey 2008 Report to Congress*, EPA-832-R-10-002 (Washington, D.C.: 2008).

but a strong scientific consensus has emerged in recent years from the U.S. Global Change Research Program and the National Research Council that the future likely entails greater risks of flooding, drought, and changes in the frequency and severity of storms.[66] In addition, several organizations have predicted specific effects of climate change in the Great Lakes, which could negatively affect GLRI restoration efforts, such as to remove contaminated sediments from areas of concern or reduce the introduction of invasive species. For example, according to a 2000 report by the U.S. Global Change Research Program, drought could lead to certain situations in the Great Lakes that may require additional dredging of sediments at an annual cost of from $75 million to $125 million—about $101.6 million to $129.6 million in 2013 dollars—simply to maintain shipping lanes.[67] In addition, the U.S. Global Change Research Program reported in 2009 that warming water temperatures can lead to increased numbers of aquatic invasive species, which tend to thrive under a wide range of environmental conditions, and a decline in native species, which are adapted to a narrower range of conditions.[68] As we noted previously, invasive species such as the zebra mussel have caused extensive ecological and economic damage to the Great Lakes.

One way to reduce the potential effects of climate change is to invest in enhancing resilience. As defined by the National Academies, resilience is the ability to prepare and plan for, absorb, recover from, and more successfully adapt to adverse events.[69] Enhanced resilience results from better planning to reduce losses, rather than waiting for an event to occur

---

[66]The U.S. Global Change Research Program coordinates and integrates the activities of 13 federal agencies that conduct research on changes in the global environment and their implications for society. For more information about the U.S. Global Change Research Program click http://www.globalchange.gov/.

[67]U.S. Global Change Research Program, Great Lakes Regional Assessment Group, *Preparing for Climate Change, The Potential Consequences of Climate Variability and Change* (Ann Arbor, MI: October 2000). The range of $75 million to $125 million was calculated based on average dredging costs at the time of at least $10 to $12 per cubic yard—about $14 to $16 per cubic yard in 2013 dollars—in a situation with heightened demand for dredging services and 7.5 million cubic yards to 12.5 million cubic removed annually.

[68]U.S. Global Change Research Program, *Global Climate Change Impacts in the United States* (New York, NY: 2009).

[69]The National Academies, Committee on Increasing National Resilience to Hazards and Disasters; Committee on Science, Engineering, and Public Policy; *Disaster Resilience: A National Imperative* (Washington, D.C.: 2012).

and paying for recovery afterward. Many jurisdictions in the Great Lakes region have recognized the threat of climate change and committed resources to prepare for its effects, according to a 2012 report focused on the region.[70] Among these efforts, several Great Lakes states and the city of Chicago have each created climate change action plans that identify steps being taken to reduce the effects of climate change. For example, the city of Chicago identified the use of green roofs as one of many climate change mitigation and adaptation actions in its 2008 *Chicago Climate Action Plan*.[71] In its subsequent progress report, Chicago reported that more than 4 million square feet of green roofs had been planned or completed since 2008.[72] A green roof is a vegetative layer grown on a rooftop that provides shade and removes heat from the air, reducing temperatures of the roof surface and the surrounding air. As a result, green roofs act as insulators for buildings and reduce the energy needed to provide cooling and heating, which can decrease the production of associated air pollution and greenhouse gas emissions that contribute to climate change.

In addition, some Great Lakes jurisdictions have recognized that climate change can exacerbate other factors that may limit Great Lakes restoration. As we reported in April 2013,[73] the Milwaukee Metropolitan Sewerage District officials employed what they called "green infrastructure" programs to make the district's sewer system more resilient to climate change by capturing and holding or slowing the flow of stormwater. This was done as part of broader efforts to meet growing demand for sewer capacity, and officials plan to incorporate climate change adaptation into infrastructure planning and design where it makes sense as their facilities age and are replaced over time.

---

[70]For information about climate change adaptation efforts in the Great Lakes region, see R. M. Gregg, K. M. Feifel, J. M. Kershner, and J. L. Hitt, *The State of Climate Change Adaptation in the Great Lakes Region* (Bainbridge Island, WA: EcoAdapt, 2012), accessed June 11, 2013, http://ecoadapt.org/programs/state-of-adaptation/great-lakes-region.

[71]City of Chicago, *Chicago Climate Action Plan* (Chicago, IL: Sept. 19, 2008), accessed June 20, 2013, http://www.chicagoclimateaction.org/.

[72]City of Chicago, *Chicago Climate Change Action Plan Progress Report: the First Two Years* (Chicago, IL: June 23, 2010), accessed June 20, 2013, http://www.chicagoclimateaction.org/pages/ccap_progress_report/81.php.

[73]GAO, *Climate Change: Future Federal Adaptation Efforts Could Better Support Local Infrastructure Decision Makers*, GAO-13-242 (Washington, D.C.: Apr. 12, 2013).

Action Plan Does Not Clearly Account for Key Factors That May Limit Its Success and Overall Great Lakes Restoration Progress

The Action Plan does not include goals, objectives, or measures of progress that show how the GLRI should address inadequate infrastructure, the effects of climate change, or other key factors that may limit the Action Plan's success and overall progress concerning the health of the Great Lakes ecosystem, with two exceptions.[74] In some cases, such as with inadequate infrastructure for wastewater or stormwater and atmospheric deposition of pollutants from sources outside the Great Lakes Basin, the Action Plan notes that some of these issues are addressed by other federal programs. For example, the Action Plan states that infrastructure needs will be addressed through increased funding for EPA's Clean Water State Revolving Funds, a program that provides states and local communities with independent and sustainable sources of financial assistance, such as low- or no-interest loans, to fund water quality projects identified by the states and localities. EPA reported in 2010 that the program has provided more than $74 billion for these projects since 1988.[75] As we testified in March 2013, however, wastewater infrastructure needs are made more daunting by the limited resources and budgets facing all levels of government.[76]

The Action Plan acknowledges that the effects of climate change may have implications across all five of the Action Plan's focus areas, and that the needs of communities to adapt to those effects will be assessed and addressed by GLRI projects and programs where appropriate. However, the Action Plan does not state how these effects will be addressed. To date, EPA has made some modest efforts to acknowledge the issue in the context of the Great Lakes. In its 2012 request for grant applications, for example, EPA included $200,000 for two to five grants for projects to increase climate change resiliency in Great Lakes communities. EPA also

---

[74]One long-term goal and one objective in the Action Plan address the key factor of insufficient coordination between the United States and Canada. The goal is that work under the goals and objectives of the Great Lakes Water Quality Agreement is coordinated between the United States and Canada through Lakewide Management Plans and other binational processes. The objective is that, by 2012, improved coordination with Canada will take place for programs under the Great Lakes Water Quality Agreement, particularly under the Lakewide Management Plans, which will result in the achievement of five to ten priority Lakewide Management Plans goals and actions.

[75]EPA, *Clean Water State Revolving Fund Programs 2009 Annual Report*, EPA-832-R-10-001 (Washington, D.C.: June 2010).

[76]GAO, *Water Infrastructure: Approaches and Issues for Financing Drinking Water and Wastewater Infrastructure*, GAO-13-451T (Washington, D.C.: Mar. 13, 2013).

included an incentive in the request for applications for 2012 for the applicants to consider climate change impacts through vulnerability assessments or the integration of climate change adaptation measures into their project. Specifically, applicants could increase their eligibility for a grant by addressing climate change in their proposal.

The GLRI was created to accelerate the protection, maintenance, and restoration of the integrity of the Great Lakes. If the Action Plan does not state how the GLRI should address key factors—such as inadequate infrastructure and the effects of climate change—then the ability of restoration efforts guided by the Action Plan to achieve the GLRI's goal is uncertain because these factors may negatively affect restoration efforts. EPA has acknowledged that the effects of climate change can be detrimental to the Great Lakes and stated in its fiscal year 2013 budget justification that it is imperative that consideration of climate change and climate adaptation be integrated into GLRI grants and projects to ensure the overall success of the GLRI.[77] Nonetheless, to date, EPA has made few connections between this key issue and the potential effects of climate change. At a series of public meetings and webinars beginning in May 2013, EPA requested input regarding whether the connection between the Action Plan focus areas and the protection of the Great Lakes from the effects of climate change should be expressed more clearly in the next Action Plan. In commenting on a draft of this report, EPA officials told us that they have heard from many stakeholders about the need for the fiscal year 2015 to 2019 Action Plan to place additional emphasis on climate change, and that there is broad agreement on this point among the task force agencies.

Conclusions

As directed by Congress, EPA and the other Task Force agencies began implementing the GLRI in fiscal year 2010 to address the stresses that threaten the health of the Great Lakes ecosystem and help restore the health of the Great Lakes and issued the GLRI Action Plan to guide implementation of the approximately $1.3 billion appropriated to the program. A collaborative and comprehensive approach, it is clear that both federal and nonfederal GLRI stakeholders believe that the program is making strides toward its goals. For example, GLRI efforts enabled EPA to remove the Presque Isle Bay area of concern from the list of

---

[77]EPA, *Fiscal Year 2013 Justification of Appropriation Estimates for the Committee on Appropriations*, EPA-190-R-12-001 (Washington, D.C.: 2012).

areas of concern identified by the United States and Canada. Nonetheless, the threats to the Great Lakes persist, and EPA and the other Task Force agencies face significant challenges in ensuring the future success of the GLRI due to issues involving their abilities to assess and achieve progress. EPA and the Task Force agencies are currently obtaining input for the next version of the GLRI Action Plan for fiscal years 2015 to 2019.

EPA has assessed GLRI progress primarily by using information from various sources to determine whether the GLRI is meeting the annual targets for the 28 measures in the Action Plan. Assessments of GLRI progress could help GLRI stakeholders, Congress, and the public discern the extent to which the health of the Great Lakes ecosystem has been restored, as well as what has been achieved by the approximately $1.3 billion appropriated to the program since fiscal year 2010. Moreover, such assessments can be used by EPA and the Task Force agencies to assess the effectiveness of GLRI actions and adjust their efforts if needed. However, we believe EPA is not well positioned to produce comprehensive and useful assessments for several reasons. Specifically:

- Some of the Action Plan's long-term goals and objectives do not have measures of progress that link to them. We believe that clear linkages between a plan's goals, objectives, and measures are critical to achieving and assessing progress over time. Without such linkages in the current Action Plan, it is unclear how EPA will be able to assess progress in meeting the Action Plan's long-term goals and objectives.

- Similarly, without identifying linkages between long-term goals, objectives, and measures in the Action Plan for 2015 to 2019 now under development, it is unclear how EPA will be able assess progress in meeting the long-term goals and objectives in that plan.

- The measures of progress do not capture the results of many of the GLRI projects because more than half of the projects are not associated with an Action Plan measure of progress in GLAS, which is a mechanism EPA created for collecting information to monitor GLRI projects and progress. We recognize that some projects do not directly provide data for any of the Action Plan's 28 measures, and that the cumulative results of some of the projects without assigned measures may ultimately be captured by some of the existing measures. With so many instances in which a project does not have an assigned measure, it is unclear if EPA will have the information it needs to capture the results of these projects and, therefore, if the agency can assess the full extent of progress being made.

- GLRI projects may directly address multiple measures of progress, but GLAS limits users to reporting the information for just one measure for each project even if more measures are being addressed. Without complete progress information on GLRI projects, the data EPA is using for certain measures of progress cannot be complete, and EPA may be underreporting GLRI progress. EPA officials told us that they will consider addressing this limitation in GLAS, but they did not specify a time frame for doing so.

- Some Action Plan measures or targets may not be useful because, among other things, they track activities that may not be sufficient to lead to the desired GLRI goals. Without useful measures, EPA may not be able to determine that GLRI efforts are producing the desired results.

- EPA and the Task Force agencies have not fully established an adaptive management plan. Although there is no requirement that the Task Force agencies establish an adaptive management plan for the GLRI, EPA and several of the Task Force agencies agreed in a 2000 to incorporate adaptive management principles into their programs. EPA and the Task Force agencies recently issued a plan that includes most but not all of the key elements of adaptive management, and it does not provide details on how the elements of adaptive management will be implemented. Without a fully established adaptive management plan, EPA and the other Task Force agencies may be limited in their ability to assess the effectiveness of GLRI efforts and adjust future actions to achieve the goals and objectives of the GLRI as results and ecosystem processes become better understood.

We recognize the potentially significant contributions that individual GLRI projects can make to resolving specific environmental and public health stresses that threaten the Great Lakes. However, we believe that these contributions need to be viewed in the context of larger factors affecting the Great Lakes, in order to more fully appreciate the long-term future of the Great Lakes and to develop optimal strategies to help ensure the best possible outcome. Some of these factors can lead to problems that will be very expensive to address. Most notably, inadequate infrastructure for wastewater and stormwater and the effects of climate change may lead to conditions that can negatively affect GLRI restoration efforts. One way to reduce the potential impacts of climate change is to invest in planning to reduce losses, rather than waiting for an event to occur and paying for recovery afterward. The Action Plan touches on these factors, but it does not directly address how these factors may affect GLRI efforts to restore the health of the Great Lakes ecosystem or provide strategies to address them. Without more clearly expressing that connection in the next Action Plan, EPA will not be able to help address the effects of these factors, including climate change, on GLRI restoration efforts.

Recommendations for Executive Action

To address challenges the Task Force faces in producing comprehensive and useful assessments of progress and addressing factors that may limit GLRI progress, we recommend that the EPA Administrator, in coordination with the Task Force, as appropriate, take the following seven actions:

- ensure progress toward long-term goals or objectives that are identified in the Action Plan, but which do not have measures that link to them, is assessed;

- ensure that linkages between long-term goals, objectives, and measures are identified in the Action Plan for 2015 to 2019;

- ensure that the progress being made by projects that do not have an Action Plan measure assigned to them is captured in assessments of GLRI progress;

- capture complete information about progress for each of the measures that are addressed by a project;

- further evaluate the usefulness of the current measures and targets and the need, if any, for the creation of additional measures;

- establish an adaptive management plan that includes all of the key elements of adaptive management and provides details on how these elements will be implemented; and

- address how factors outside of the scope of the Action Plan that may limit progress, such as inadequate infrastructure for wastewater or stormwater and the effects of climate change, may affect GLRI efforts to restore the Great Lakes.

Agency Comments and Our Evaluation

We provided a draft of this report to EPA, the Departments of Agriculture, Commerce, Defense, Health and Human Services, Homeland Security, the Interior, State, and Transportation, and the Council on Environmental Quality for comment. In written comments from the EPA Region 5 Administrator, which are reproduced in appendix II, EPA generally agreed with the conclusions and recommendations in our report. EPA noted in particular that our report is well-timed because it comes at the beginning of a new 5-year GLRI planning cycle. The agency also noted that we rightly acknowledged the complexity of assessing and quantifying overall Great Lakes health, the difficulty of attributing specific environmental changes to specific projects or programs, and the slow pace of ecosystem change.

In addition, EPA noted that the agency is already taking actions consistent with our recommendations, including working to develop more appropriate measures of progress in the Action Plan for fiscal years 2015 to 2019 and finalizing the draft framework. The agency also noted it is working with the task force agencies to link all activities described in interagency agreements to goals, objectives, and measures of progress in the Action Plan to help to track projects where there is not currently an associated measure of progress for which data can be reported in GLAS. EPA also noted that the agency has heard from many stakeholders about the need for the next Action Plan to place additional emphasis on climate change, and that there is broad agreement on this point from Task Force agencies. Taken together, we believe comprehensive actions along the lines stated in the EPA letter would constitute important steps forward, and we will look forward to seeing the progress the agency has made in taking these actions in the 2015 to 2019 Action Plan.

In written comments from the Department of the Interior's Assistant Secretary for Policy, Management, and Budget, which are reproduced in appendix III, Interior noted that information in our report is accurate and relevant, and the agency acknowledged the challenges in quantifying the progress toward restoration goals that we identified in our report. The Department of Agriculture provided technical comments but did not comment on our recommendations. Its letter is reproduced in appendix IV.

In addition to these written comments, the Council on Environmental Quality submitted an e-mail on September 13, 2013, that further emphasized our findings on the need for accountability. Specifically, this e-mail stated that GLAS limitations have led to an underreporting of progress for certain measures, so that they are not most accurately reflecting what benefits are accruing under the measures and projects implemented. EPA and the Departments of Agriculture, the Interior, and Transportation, provided technical comments that we incorporated as appropriate.

As agreed with your offices, unless you publicly announce the contents of this report earlier, we plan no further distribution until 30 days from the report date. At that time, we will send copies to the Administrator of the EPA, the appropriate congressional committees, and other interested parties. In addition, the report will be available at no charge on the GAO website at http://www.gao.gov.

If you or your staff members have any questions about this report, please contact me at (202) 512-3841 or gomezj@gao.gov. Contact points for our Offices of Congressional Relations and Public Affairs may be found on the last page of this report. GAO staff who made significant contributions to this report are listed in appendix VII.

J. Alfredo Gómez
Director, Natural Resources and Environment

Appendix I: Objectives, Scope, and Methodology

This appendix provides information on the scope of work and the methodology used to examine (1) how the Great Lakes Restoration Initiative (GLRI) is implemented by the Task Force agencies and other stakeholders; (2) the methods that the Environmental Protection Agency (EPA) has in place to assess GLRI progress; (3) the progress identified by the Task Force agencies and nonfederal stakeholders; and (4) the views of nonfederal stakeholders on factors, if any, that may affect or limit GLRI progress.

To examine how the GLRI is implemented by the Great Lakes Interagency Task Force (Task Force) agencies and other stakeholders we analyzed key documents and interviewed individuals involved with the GLRI.[1] Specifically, we analyzed the *Great Lakes Restoration Initiative Action Plan Fiscal Years 2010-2014* (Action Plan) to understand its structure and identify the long-term goals, objectives, measures of progress and related annual targets, and principal actions in each of the Action Plan's five focus areas;[2] EPA GLRI financial reports and the agency's fiscal year 2014 budget justification to determine the amount of GLRI funds that have been allocated for fiscal years 2010 to 2013 to each Task Force agency and each focus area; and, information from the Great Lakes Accountability System (GLAS) to identify the number of GLRI projects in each focus area and to learn more about GLRI projects, such as location, size, and funding.[3] We also reviewed interagency

---

[1]The Task Force is chaired by the EPA Administrator, and includes senior officials from the U.S. Departments of Agriculture, Commerce, Defense, Health and Human Services, Homeland Security, Housing and Urban Development, the Interior, State, and Transportation and the White House Council on Environmental Quality. The subagencies within the Task Force agencies that are responsble for implementing the GLRI are: the Department of Agriculture's Animal and Plant Health Inspection Service, Forest Service, and Natural Resources Conservation Service; the Department of Commerce's National Oceanic and Atmospheric Administration; the Department of Defense's U.S. Army Corps of Engineers; the Department of Health and Human Services' Agency for Toxic Substances and Disease Registry; the Department of Homeland Security's Coast Guard; the Department of the Interior's Bureau of Indian Affairs, Fish and Wildlife Service, National Park Service, and U.S. Geological Survey; and the Department of Transportation's Federal Highway Administration and Maritime Administration. We refer to all 16 Task Force agencies and subagencies collectively as Task Force agencies in this report, as is the case on the GLRI website http://greatlakesrestoration.us/priorities.html.

[2]Great Lakes Interagency Task Force, *Great Lakes Restoration Initiative Action Plan Fiscal Years 2010-2014* (Washington, D.C.: Feb. 21, 2010).

[3]GLAS is a mechanism for collecting information to monitor GLRI projects and progress and was created by EPA.

agreements between EPA and the Task Force agencies that identify the amount of GLRI funds EPA will allocate to each agency and the GLRI projects the agencies will implement. In addition, we conducted interviews with federal stakeholders, officials from EPA headquarters, EPA's office responsible for implementing the GLRI, the Great Lakes National Program Office, and the other Task Force agencies. We also interviewed representatives from nonfederal GLRI stakeholders—such as the Nature Conservancy and the Great Lakes Indian Fish and Wildlife Commission[4]—and a prominent Great Lakes interest group, Healing Our Waters – Great Lakes Coalition, to gain an understanding of the GLRI and how it is implemented.[5] Nonfederal stakeholders are state and local governments, tribes, nongovernmental organizations, and academic institutions that have received GLRI funds. We also attended the Eighth Annual Great Lakes Restoration Conference in Cleveland in September 2012 to learn more about the GLRI and Great Lakes restoration, and webinars to learn about the GLRI grant application process and how to use GLAS.

To examine the methods that EPA has in place to assess GLRI progress, we analyzed the Action Plan, documentation about GLAS, information from GLAS about GLRI project measures of progress,[6] information provided by EPA on the sources of data for each of the plan's measures of progress, the draft *GLRI Adaptive Science-Based Framework for Great Lakes Restoration* (draft Framework), and EPA's Science Advisory Board's 2012 review of the Action Plan.[7] We interviewed EPA officials to

---

[4]The Nature Conservancy is a nonprofit conservation organization that works to protect ecologically important lands and water for nature and people, and the Great Lakes Indian Fish and Wildlife Commission provides natural resource management expertise and conservation enforcement, among other things, in support of the 11 Great Lakes tribes it represents.

[5]The Healing Our Waters – Great Lakes Coalition consists of more than 120 environmental, conservation, and outdoor recreation organizations, zoos, aquariums and museums, and works to secure a sustainable Great Lakes restoration plan and implement it.

[6]We reviewed GLAS, and not the other sources of progress information—such as from other federal agencies, states, and universities—because EPA officials told us that it is the only new database created by EPA for the purpose of assessing GLRI progress. We did not use information in GLAS that was entered by users for the purpose of describing progress made by GLRI projects because of concerns raised by EPA about the quality of that information.

[7]EPA Science Advisory Board, *Review of Great Lakes Restoration Initiative Action Plan* (Washington, D.C.: Jan. 24, 2012).

discuss their methods of assessing GLRI progress. We used the interviews with Task Force agency officials described above, and we conducted interviews with relevant officials from each of the Great Lakes states—Illinois, Indiana, Michigan, Minnesota, New York, Ohio, Pennsylvania, and Wisconsin—to discuss the Action Plan. We also conducted interviews with subject matter experts, to obtain their views about the achievability and usefulness of the Action Plan's measures of progress and related annual targets.

As part of our analysis of the Action Plan, we evaluated the extent to which the long-term goals and objectives in the plan have corresponding measures of progress. One analyst first compared the objectives for each focus area with the goals. The analyst considered whether it appeared that an objective would clearly contribute to attaining a goal. For example, in the invasive species focus area, the objective of developing and refining/piloting technologies that contain or control invasive species appears to clearly contribute to attaining the goal of preventing the spread of invasive species. The analyst also considered whether there was consistent or similar language in any of the goals and objectives that helped identify links between them. For example, the analysts examined if aspects of a goal in one focus area could be identified in an objective in the same focus area, such as in the toxic substances and areas of concern focus area, we identified similar language between the objective of reducing the concentrations of polychlorinated biphenyls (PCBs) in fish through 2014 and the goal of reducing environmental levels of toxic chemicals to the point that all restrictions on the consumption of Great Lakes fish can be lifted. Objectives could correspond to multiple goals. The analyst then compared the measures for each focus area to the objectives and looked for consistent or similar language in any of them that helped identify links between the objectives and measures. The analyst considered whether a measure was closely related to an objective and whether it appeared that progress toward at least part of the objective could clearly be assessed by a corresponding measure of progress. Measures could correspond to multiple objectives. We requested additional information from EPA officials on goals, objectives, and measures as needed to improve our understanding of them. A second analyst examined the conclusions of the first. In cases where there were initially disagreements between the two analysts regarding the identification of linkages between goals, objectives, and measures, all disagreements were resolved through analyst discussions. Ultimately, there was 100 percent agreement between the analysts. In addition, we evaluated the extent to which EPA and the Task Force agencies had established an adaptive management plan for the GLRI by first reviewing guidance from several Task Force agencies to identify key elements of adaptive management. We then examined the extent to which the GLRI Action Plan and draft Framework addressed those elements.

For our interviews with officials from each of the Great Lakes states, we developed a set list of open-ended questions for these interviews to obtain official's views about the Action Plan, among other things. We identified the state agencies that we would contact by starting with the list of state agencies identified at EPA's Great Lakes website as interested parties.[8] We then contacted officials from each interested party to determine if their agency was the lead GLRI agency for the state or to learn if we should contact a different agency. As a result of this process, we identified the following as lead GLRI state agencies: the Illinois Department of Natural Resources; the Indiana Department of Environmental Management; the Michigan Department of Environmental Quality; the Minnesota Pollution Control Agency; the New York Department of Environmental Conservation; the Ohio Lake Erie Commission; the Pennsylvania Department of Environmental Protection; and, the Wisconsin Department of Natural Resources.

For the interviews with subject matter experts, we developed a set list of questions about the Action Plan's long-term goals, objectives, and measures of progress. The experts we interviewed included state agency officials, members of academia, and representatives of nongovernmental organizations who had expertise in one or more of the Action Plan's five focus areas. We identified these experts by asking for recommendations of at least three experts in each of the focus areas from 24 representatives of nonfederal Great Lakes stakeholders or Great Lakes interest groups organizations: 12 were nonfederal attendees of the Eighth Annual Great Lakes Restoration Conference that we selected randomly to conduct interviews about the Action Plan and the GLRI, and 12 were representatives of nonfederal organizations that we contacted as part of

---

[8]For EPA's list of Great Lakes interested parties, click http://www.epa.gov/greatlakes/parties/states.html.

learning more about the GLRI and the Great Lakes.[9] We received responses from 17 of the 24 individuals who recommended a total of 187 subject matter experts.[10] We then created a list of the 33 experts who had been recommended two or more times and invited 31 of them to participate in interviews to obtain their views on the Action Plan goals, objectives, and measures of progress, among other things.[11] Of those 31 experts, 21 agreed to be interviewed: five experts in focus area one; six experts in focus area two; three experts in focus area three; four experts in focus area four; and three experts in focus area five. Because we used a nonprobability sample, the information obtained from these interviews is not generalizable to other individuals with expertise in the Action Plan focus areas but provides illustrative information.

To examine the progress identified by the Task Force agencies and nonfederal stakeholders, we took several steps: we reviewed the fiscal year 2010 and 2011 GLRI progress reports that EPA and the other Task Force agencies issued to Congress in April and March 2013, respectively;[12] we administered a web-based survey to each of the 205 nonfederal stakeholders that, as of October 2012, had received GLRI funds from a Task Force agency and had a project identified in GLAS; we used the interviews with officials from each Task Force agency identified above; and, we visited several GLRI projects in Illinois.

---

[9]We conducted interviews with 19 randomly selected, nonfederal individuals at the conference. These individuals were either representatives of nonfederal GLRI stakeholders or Great Lakes interest groups. The number of conference attendees we were able to interview was determined by the number of attendees who were available at the times that we sought out interviewees and were in same location of where we sought out interviewees, and the willingness of the attendees we approached to participate in the interview. Twelve of these individuals recommended subject matter experts.

[10]One of the 17 individuals recommended 21 subject matter experts in a focus area.

[11]We did not invite two subject matters experts to participate. This is because one expert had already provided a lot of information to this report, and we wanted to minimize the response burden. In addition, another expert had demonstrated in a previous interview that he shared the same opinions as a subject matter expert in the same focus area who works for the same organization and who we had already interviewed, and we wanted to minimize the likelihood of duplicate responses. In each case, we interviewed four or more other experts in the relevant focus areas.

[12]EPA in partnership with the Great Lakes Interagency Task Force, *Great Lakes Restoration Initiative Fiscal Year 2010 Report to Congress and the President*, (Washington, D.C.: March 2011), and EPA in partnership with the Great Lakes Interagency Task Force, Great Lakes Restoration Initiative Fiscal Year 2011 Report to Congress and the President (Washington, D.C.: September 2011).

We conducted a web-based survey of all of the nonfederal GLRI
stakeholders that have reported projects in GLAS, as of October 10,
2012, to identify examples of GLRI progress by obtaining their views on
how their GLRI projects have benefited the ecosystem, among other
things. The questionnaire used for this study is in appendix V. EPA
provided us with contact information for each of those stakeholders, and
we sent at least one e-mail to a point of contact from each stakeholder to
identify the best point of contact for our survey. We surveyed the universe
of the 205 nonfederal stakeholders that have projects in GLAS, as of
October 10, 2012, and received responses from 176 nonfederal GLRI
stakeholders for a response rate of 86 percent.

We designed draft questionnaires in close collaboration with a GAO
social science survey specialist. We conducted pretests with three
nonfederal GLRI stakeholders to help further refine our questions,
develop new questions, and clarify any ambiguous portions of the survey.
We conducted the pretests over the phone, and we selected one GLRI
nonfederal stakeholder that had received GLRI funds for one grant and
two GLRI nonfederal stakeholders that had each received GLRI funds for
multiple grants for the pretest.

We developed and administered the web-based questionnaire accessible
through a secure server, and we e-mailed unique identification numbers
and passwords to points of contact at the 205 nonfederal GLRI
stakeholders February 4, 2013. We sent follow-up e-mail messages
beginning February 11, 2013. Then we contacted all remaining
nonrespondents by telephone, starting February 26, 2013. The
questionnaire was available online until March 28, 2013. For questions
that should have been skipped but were not, we attempted to contact the
respondents for clarification and edited their responses where warranted.

Because this was not a sample survey, it has no sampling errors.
However, the practical difficulties of conducting any survey may introduce
errors, known as nonsampling errors. For example, difficulties in
interpreting a particular question, sources of information available to
respondents, or when entering data into a questionnaire or analyzing the
data can introduce unwanted variability into the survey results. We took
steps in developing our questionnaire, collecting the data, and analyzing it
to minimize these errors. In addition, as indicated above, social science
survey specialists designed the questionnaire in collaboration with GAO
staff that had subject matter expertise. We then conducted three pretests
to check that (1) the questions were clear and unambiguous, (2)
terminology was used correctly, (3) the questionnaire did not place an

undue burden on respondents, (4) the information could feasibly be obtained, and (5) the survey was comprehensive and unbiased. We made multiple contact attempts with nonrespondents during the survey by e-mail, and some nonrespondents were also contacted by telephone. When we analyzed the data, an independent analyst checked all computer programs. Since this was a web-based survey, respondents entered their answers directly into the electronic questionnaire, eliminating the need to key data into a database, minimizing error.

We conducted a computer-enabled content analysis to analyze responses to the question "Please provide examples of how one or more of your organization's GLRI projects have benefitted the Great Lakes ecosystem." Of the 176 respondents, 163 provided information in response to this question. We categorized the responses along two dimensions: direct and indirect benefits, and observed or expected benefits. We defined these categories based on whether respondents reported that their organization's GLRI projects resulted in changes in the ecosystem, such as reduced beach closure days, or other types of changes, such as improved understanding of the ecosystem, and if respondents reported that they had observed the result or expected to observe them a later time. One reviewer developed content categories based on survey responses and, after obtaining agreement on the categories from the second reviewer, assessed and coded each survey response into those categories. The second reviewer examined the coding. In cases where disagreements among the two reviewers regarding the coding of responses into content categories were found, all disagreements were resolved through reviewer discussion. Ultimately, there was 100 percent agreement between the reviewers. In addition, we conducted follow-up interviews by phone and e-mail with those survey respondents whose examples we wanted to include in the report to collect clarifying information, if necessary.

In addition to the survey, we used the interviews with Task Force agency officials identified above to obtain information about GLRI progress. We also visited several GLRI projects in Illinois. We traveled to Illinois because EPA's Great Lakes National Program Office is located in Chicago. We met with representatives from two nonfederal GLRI stakeholders who took us to the sites of their GLRI projects; the two nonfederal GLRI stakeholders—the Chicago Park District and Waukegan Harbor Citizens Advisory Group—were recommended to us by an official from the Illinois Department of Natural Resources.

To examine the views of nonfederal stakeholders on factors, if any, that may affect or limit GLRI progress, we used the web-based survey described above. Specifically, we used the survey to obtain nonfederal GLRI stakeholder views about factors that may have limited their ability to carry out GLRI projects and factors that have the potential to affect the restoration of Great Lakes health. As part of creating the survey, we developed lists of factors that might limit GLRI project implementation progress and factors that might limit the restoration of Great Lakes health in general through interviews we conducted with 19 randomly selected individuals at the Eight Annual Great Lakes Restoration Conference and interviews we conducted with representatives from five nonfederal GLRI stakeholders and one Great Lakes interest group. We narrowed the list of factors that might limit GLRI project implementation progress to four factors most often cited by interviewees as hindering their abilities to start a project or to successfully carry out a project, and asked survey respondents if they had experienced these factors and about the effects of each of these factors on their GLRI projects. We narrowed the list of factors that might limit the restoration of Great Lakes health in general to the nine factors most often cited by grouping similar factors together and eliminating those factors that are addressed by the Action Plan either through Action Plan long-term goals, objectives, or measures of progress. We eliminated those factors addressed by the Action Plan because this meant they had already been identified by the GLRI as factors that had the potential to limit restoration of Great Lakes health. We asked survey respondents to identify the extent to which each of these factors had the potential to limit the restoration of the health of the Great Lakes ecosystem.

We also used the interviews with subject matter experts mentioned above to obtain information about the factors that may limit progress by asking them to identify the extent to which each of the same nine factors we included in the survey had the potential to limit the restoration of the health of the Great Lakes ecosystem.

We conducted this performance audit from June 2012 to September 2013 in accordance with generally accepted government auditing standards. Those standards require that we plan and perform the audit to obtain sufficient, appropriate evidence to provide a reasonable basis for our findings and conclusions based on our audit objectives. We believe that the evidence obtained provides a reasonable basis for our findings and conclusions based on our audit objectives.

Appendix II: Comments from the Environment Protection Agency

United States Environmental Protection Agency
Regional Administrator
Region 5
77 West Jackson Boulevard
Chicago, IL 60604-3590

SEP 1 1 2013

Mr. Alfredo Gomez
Acting Director
Natural Resources and Environment
U.S. Government Accountability Office
Washington, DC 20548

Dear Mr. Gomez:

Thank you for the opportunity to review and comment on the GAO Draft Report, *Great Lakes Restoration Initiative: Further Actions Would Result in More Useful Assessments and Help Address Factors That Limit Progress* (GAO-13-797). The U.S. Environmental Protection Agency appreciates your staff's impressive effort to learn about the scope and complexities of this new initiative and to understand the challenges associated with coordinating the work of 16 federal agencies involved in GLRI implementation.

EPA generally agrees with the conclusions and recommendations contained in GAO's Draft Report and, in many cases, EPA is already taking action that is consistent with the recommendations:

- The GAO recommendations concerning the need for improved assessment of GLRI progress are consistent with steps already being taken as GLRI agencies work to improve existing information systems and to develop more appropriate measures of progress in the FY15-19 GLRI Action Plan.
- The GAO recommendation concerning the importance of adaptive management is consistent with steps already being taken as GLRI agencies work to finalize an *Adaptive Science-Based Framework for Great Lakes Restoration.*
- The GAO recommendation regarding the need to account for climate change and other factors outside of the scope of the FY10-14 Action Plan that may limit GLRI progress is already a major focus of discussions underway to develop the FY15-19 GLRI Action Plan.

This GAO Report is particularly well-timed – because it comes at the beginning of a new 5-year GLRI planning cycle. On March 6, 2013, the Chair of the White House Council on Environmental Quality, announced the Administration's commitment to an updated 5-year GLRI Action Plan. Since then, the GLRI agencies have been working to gather input to be used to develop an FY15-19 Action Plan that will increase the effectiveness of GLRI investments – and we have already received comments from a wide range of stakeholders that mirror some of GAO's recommendations:

- A Great Lakes Advisory Board, a Federal Advisory Committee, was constituted on March 13, 2013. The GLAB supports GLRI implementation by providing advice to the EPA Administrator in her capacity as Interagency Task Force chair. The scientists, business leaders, public servants, and non-profit organization representatives on the GLAB have already held multiple public meetings and are expected to issue an Advisory Report in the coming months.

Recycled/Recyclable · Printed with Vegetable Oil Based Inks on 100% Recycled Paper (50% post Consumer)

- The IATF hosted a series of stakeholder engagement opportunities from May through July, 2013, including three public meetings (NY, WI, and OH), two webinars, several conference calls, and a public comment period (http://glri.us/comment.html).

- The IATF posted a Draft *Adaptive Science-Based Framework for Great Lakes Restoration* online for public comment in May 2013. The *Framework* is intended to guide cost-effective and strategically appropriate GLRI restoration actions, using the best available science and applying lessons learned from past and on-going restoration projects and programs. In the coming months, the GLRI agencies expect to finalize the *Adaptive Science-Based Framework for Great Lakes Restoration.*

We have heard from many stakeholders about the need for the FY15-19 Action Plan to place additional emphasis on climate change – and there is broad agreement on this point among the GLRI agencies. In the meantime, EPA continues to build on our initial efforts to address climate change cited in the Draft Report (pg. 51) and to work with other GLRI agencies to document climate-related considerations in the statements of work required for interagency agreements. EPA is also working with GLRI agencies to link all activities described in statements of work to goals, objectives and measures of progress in the Action Plan. This will help to track projects where there is not currently an associated measure of progress for which data can be reported in the Great Lakes Accountability System database – an issue discussed in the Draft Report (pg. 18.)

Finally, there are two critical points about the GLRI and overall Great Lakes restoration efforts that deserve special emphasis:

- The GLRI was created to *accelerate* the protection, maintenance, and restoration of the Great Lakes. The Great Lakes community – private landowners, industry and business, academia, nongovernmental organizations, tribes, municipalities, state and federal government – each have a unique and active role in overall Great Lakes restoration efforts. The GLRI is intended to *supplement* longstanding federal government Great Lakes programs. As such, the purpose of the GLRI is to achieve faster and more effective progress than would otherwise be accomplished. GLRI is not, however, intended to accelerate every federal program that furthers restoration of the Great Lakes. Traditional (gray) infrastructure and Superfund cleanups, for example, are outside the scope of the GLRI -- but are nonetheless critical to overall efforts to restore the Great Lakes. For information about the relative contribution of the GLRI, please see the Office of Management and Budget's annual Great Lakes crosscut budget.

- GAO rightly acknowledges the complexity of assessing and quantifying overall Great Lakes health, the difficulty of attributing specific environmental changes to specific projects or programs, and the slow pace of ecosystem change. Nevertheless, it is important to recognize that the Great Lakes community continues to work to better assess and quantify overall Great Lakes health. Many parties are engaged in significant efforts to develop and refine a set of comprehensive, basin-wide indicators to track the health of the Great Lakes. In addition, the 2012 revisions to the Great Lakes Water Quality Agreement require binational reporting on environmental conditions in the Great Lakes every three years. These efforts will continue to have an important role in gauging the overall health of the Great Lakes.

The GLRI agencies expect to issue a Draft FY15-19 Action Plan for public comment sometime after the
release of the President's FY15 Budget. I can assure you that Draft will reflect GAO's timely
recommendations -- and will be better because of GAO's input. We sincerely appreciate GAO's efforts
to help improve the effectiveness of the GLRI.

Should you have any questions about this letter or the appended technical comments, please don't
hesitate to contact me or Christopher Korleski, Director of the Great Lakes National Program Office,
Korleski.christopher@epa.gov (312-353-8320).

Sincerely,

Susan Hedman
Great Lakes National Program Manager
Regional Administrator, Region 5

Enclosure: Suggested Technical Changes

cc: EPA GAO Liaison Team
        Cameron Davis, Senior Advisor to the Administrator

Appendix III: Comments from the Department of the Interior

United States Department of the Interior

OFFICE OF THE SECRETARY
Washington, D.C. 20240

SEP 17 2013

Mr. J. Alfredo Gomez
Director, Natural Resources and Environment
U.S. Government Accountability Office
441 G Street, N.W.
Washington, D.C. 20548

Dear Mr. Gomez:

Thank you for providing the Department of the Interior the opportunity to review and comment on the draft Government Accountability Office Report entitled *GREAT LAKES RESTORATION INITIATIVE: Further Actions Would Result in More Useful Assessments and Help Address Factors That Limit Progress* (GAO-13-797).

Information presented as background, as well as the characterization of the interagency process by which funds are allocated to implement the Great Lakes Restoration Initiative (GLRI) activities (according to the Action Plan), is relevant and accurate. In general, we acknowledge the challenges in quantifying the progress towards restoration goals that the Report identifies, and do not disagree with those findings.

Enclosed for consideration as the final report is prepared are Interior's general comments. If you have any questions, or need additional information, contact Lindy Nelson, Office of Environmental Policy and Compliance, at (215) 597-5012.

Sincerely,

Rhea Suh
Assistant Secretary
Policy, Management and Budget

Enclosure

Appendix IV: Comments from the Department of Agriculture

United States Department of Agriculture

Office of the Secretary
Washington, D.C. 20250
SEP 2 0 2013

Mr. J. Alfredo Gomez
Director
Natural Resources and Environment
Government Accountability Office
441 G Street, N.W.
Washington, D.C. 20548

Dear Mr. Gomez:

Thank you for your letter of August 16, 2013, to Secretary Thomas J. Vilsack, regarding the Department of Agriculture's comments on the draft report entitled, *Great Lakes Restoration Initiative: Further Actions Would Result in More Useful Assessments and Help Address Factors That Limit Progress*, (GAO-13-797).

The Natural Resources Conservation Service (NRCS), Animal and Plant Health Inspection Service (APHIS), and Forest Service (FS) have no substantive comments. Enclosed are the NRCS technical comments to the Government Accountability Office audit report.

Again, thank you for the opportunity to comment on this report. If you require additional information, please contact Lesia A. Reed, Deputy Chief for Strategic Planning and Accountability, NRCS, at (301) 504-0056.

Sincerely,

ROBERT BONNIE
Under Secretary
Natural Resources and Environment

Enclosure

An Equal Opportunity Employer

Appendix V: Survey Questions

We conducted a web-based survey of nonfederal GLRI stakeholders that have reported projects in the Great Lakes Accountability System, as of October 10, 2012, using all of the questions below as stated here.[1] Nonfederal stakeholders are state and local governments, tribes, nongovernmental organizations, and academic institutions that that have received GLRI funds.

[1]The Great Lakes Accountability System is a mechanism for collecting information to monitor GLRI projects and progress and was created by EPA.

Survey of Great Lakes Restoration Initiative (GLRI) Grantees

United States Government Accountability Office

Introduction

The U.S. Government Accountability Office (GAO), an agency of the U.S. Congress, is conducting a review of the Great Lakes Restoration Initiative (GLRI). This review has been requested by the Chairman of the House Subcommittee on Water Resources and Environment, Committee on Transportation and Infrastructure. One of the topics we plan to address is how GLRI stakeholders characterize the extent of GLRI progress made and the factors that may limit progress. As part of addressing this topic, we are gathering information from GLRI grantees about their experiences implementing GLRI projects, strengths of the GLRI program, suggestions for improvements to the GLRI program, and Great Lakes restoration in general.

Your responses to the following questions will help us inform Congress about what is happening on the ground. We will aggregate the information that we gather through this survey in our report to Congress, and we do not plan to identify respondents beyond the type of the organizations; that is, we plan to discuss information collected from nongovernmental organizations, state agencies, tribes, academic institutions, and others. This report will be made available to the public.

To learn more about completing the survey, printing your responses, and whom to contact if you have questions, click here for help.

We appreciate you taking the time to provide your input on this.

1 of 12

Section 1 - Background

1. Please provide the following information for the primary person completing this questionnaire in the event we need to contact you to clarify a response.

Name:	
Title:	
Agency/Organization:	
E-mail:	
Telephone *(include area code)*:	

GLRI Projects Identified in the Great Lakes Accountability System for
your Organization Funded in Federal Fiscal Years 2010, 2011, or 2012

2. In the Great Lakes Accountability System, your organization is identified as having _____ GLRI projects funded in federal fiscal years 2010, 2011, or 2012. (See list of projects above.)

Is this number correct?

○ Yes
○ No

(If no) For how many GLRI projects has your organization received funding directly from federal agencies? [ ] GLRI projects

Please identify any additions or deletions of projects from the list that we included above.

2 of 12

The next set of questions in sections 2 through 5 pertain to your organization's ability to implement its GLRI projects. The focus will be on various factors that may have limited your organization's ability to carry out these projects. By limited, we mean that you were unable to implement your organization's GLRI projects as intended, such as a delayed start time or reduced scope. When answering these questions, please consider all of the GLRI projects for which you received GLRI funds directly from a federal agency in federal fiscal years 2010, 2011, and 2012.

3 of 12

Section 2 - Implementation of GLRI Projects - Quality Assurance Requirements

This section focuses on quality assurance requirements for your organization's GLRI projects.

3. Did your organization need to complete quality assurance requirements **for any** of its GLRI projects?

○ Yes
○ No

3a. (If yes) On average, approximately how long (in months) did it take for your organization to complete and submit the quality assurance requirements for its GLRI projects? *(Enter number.)*

☐ Months

3b. Did the time it took your organization to complete and submit the quality assurance requirements result in starting **any** of your projects later than originally planned?

○ Yes - *Continue with question 3c.*
○ No *(Click here to skip to question 3h)*

3c. (If yes) How many of your organization's projects were started later than originally planned due to the amount of time it took to complete and submit the quality assurance requirements? *(Enter number.)*

☐ Projects

3d. Of these projects that started later than originally planned, what was the **longest amount of time (in months) that a project start was delayed**, and in what federal fiscal year was the grant for that project awarded? *(Enter number and year.)*

Longest time a project start was delayed	☐ Months
Federal fiscal year the grant for that project was awarded	[none]

3e. Please identify which federal agency's or agencies' quality assurance requirements process resulted in starting **any** of your organization's projects later than originally planned.

☐

3f. As a result of any of the time it took your organization to complete and submit the quality assurance requirements, did your organization have to delay the start time of **any** of its GLRI projects until the following spring to wait for the ground or water to thaw?

○ Yes
○ No

3g. Has the time it has taken your organization to complete and submit quality assurance requirements decreased over time? To answer this question, please consider the time it has taken to complete and submit quality assurance requirements **for similar types of projects.**

○ Yes
○ No
○ Not applicable, our organization completed quality assurance requirements only once or for different types of projects.

4 of 12

3h. Please provide any comments you would like to make about your organization's experience with GLRI quality assurance requirements.

5 of 12

Section 3 - Implementation of GLRI Projects - Obtaining Permits

This section focuses on obtaining permits for your organization's GLRI projects.

4. Did **any** of your organization's projects need a federal, state, or local permit?

- ○ Yes
- ○ No

    4a. (If yes) On average, approximately how long (in months) did it take to obtain the necessary federal, state, or local permits for your organization's GLRI projects? *(Enter number.)*

        ☐ Months

    4b. Did the time it took to obtain the permit(s) necessary to implement your organization's GLRI projects result in starting any of your organization's projects later than originally planned?

        ○ Yes - *Continue with question 4c.*
        ○ No *(Click here to skip to question 4g)*

    4c. (If yes) How many of your organization's projects were started later than originally planned due to the amount of time it took to obtain the necessary permits? *(Enter number.)*

        ☐ Projects

    4d. Of these projects that started later than originally planned, what was the **longest amount of time (in months) that a project start was delayed**, and in what federal fiscal year was the grant for that project awarded? *(Enter number and year.)*

Longest time a project start was delayed	☐ Months
Federal fiscal year the grant for that project was awarded	[none]

    4e. What type of permit caused the delay in implementing **any** of your organization's GLRI projects? **(Select all that apply.)**

        ☐ Local permit
        ☐ State permit
        ☐ Federal permit

    4f. As a result of any of the time it took to obtain necessary permits, did your organization have to delay the start time of **any** of its GLRI projects until the following spring to wait for the ground or water to thaw?

        ○ Yes
        ○ No

    4g. Please provide any comments you would like to make about your experience obtaining permits for any of your organization's GLRI projects.

6 of 12

Section 4 - Implementation of GLRI Projects - Timing of Award Notification

This section focuses on the timing of the award notification for your organization's GLRI projects.

5. Was the start date of any of your organization's GLRI projects delayed because of the timing of when it received notice that its GLRI projects would be funded (award notification)?

○ Yes
○ No

5a. (If yes) For the projects that were delayed due to the timing of the award notification, on average, approximately how long (in months) was the interval between the time that your organization had planned to start these GLRI projects and when you actually started these GLRI projects? *(Enter number.)*

[ ] Months

5b. How many of your organization's projects were started later than originally planned due to the timing of the award notification? *(Enter number.)*

[ ] Projects

5c. Of these projects that started later than originally planned, what was the **longest amount of time (in months) that a project start was delayed**, and in what federal fiscal year was the grant for that project awarded? *(Enter number and year.)*

Longest time a project start was delayed	[ ] Months
Federal fiscal year the grant for that project was awarded	[none]

5d. As a result of the timing of the award notification, did your organization have to delay the start time of **any** of its GLRI projects until the following spring to wait for the ground or water to thaw?

○ Yes
○ No

5e. If any of your organization's projects were delayed because of the timing of award notification for reasons unrelated to seasons (as described in question 5d), please describe how the timing of award notification caused a delayed start time for one of those projects.

[ ]

6. Please provide any comments you would like to make about any aspect of the GLRI award notification process.

[ ]

7 of 12

Section 5 - Implementation of GLRI Projects - Weather and Other Factors

This section focuses on the effect of weather and other factors on your organization's GLRI projects.

7. Did **weather events** limit your organization's ability to carry out **any** of its GLRI projects in the following ways at any point during the project? **Weather events** include, but are not limited to, storms or limited rainfall, but **do not include seasons**. *(Select one answer in each row.)*

	Yes	No	Not sure
a. A weather event caused a delayed start to a GLRI project	○	○	○
b. A weather event caused a suspension of GLRI project activities for a period of time	○	○	○
c. A weather event resulted in a delayed completion of a GLRI project	○	○	○

For item a - Please describe the weather event and how it caused a delayed start to a GLRI project:	

For item b - Please describe the weather event and how it caused a suspension of GLRI project activities for a period of time:	

For item c - Please describe the weather event and how it resulted in a delayed completion of a GLRI project:	

8. Other than the factors covered in any of the previous questions on this questionnaire, were there any other factors that limited your organization's ability to implement **any** of its GLRI projects as intended?

○ Yes
○ No

8a. (If yes) Please describe these other factors and their effect on your organization's GLRI projects.

8 of 12

Section 6 - GLRI Program Benefits

This section focuses on the benefits obtained from the GLRI Program.

9. Please provide examples of things that have gone well in your organization's experience with the GLRI program. This can include, but should not be limited to, your experiences with or observations about the federal agencies administering the program as well as your own experience implementing the program.

10. Please provide examples of how one or more of your organization's GLRI projects have benefitted the community in or near the project area.

11. Please provide examples of how one or more of your organization's GLRI projects have benefitted the Great Lakes ecosystem. (For this question we are looking for a high-level description of project outcomes that we can use to illustrate how GLRI projects are helping to restore the health of the Great Lakes ecosystem. It is not necessary to provide the evidence linking your organization's GLRI project to the ecosystem benefit you have identified. We realize that benefits for many GLRI projects may not be observable or quantifiable at this time.)

9 of 12

Section 7 - Great Lakes Restoration

The two questions in this section pertain to factors outside of the scope of the GLRI Action Plan that have the potential to affect the broader goal of restoring the health of the Great Lakes ecosystem. In responding to these questions, please consider whether these factors may affect Great Lakes restoration overall and not just your organization's GLRI projects.

12. Based on your experience and given current policies affecting the Great Lakes region, to what extent do the following factors have the potential to limit the restoration of the health of the Great Lakes ecosystem? *(Select one answer in each row.)*

	To a very great extent	To a great extent	To a moderate extent	To some or little extent	To no extent	No basis to judge	Not applicable
a. Effects of climate change	○	○	○	○	○	○	○
b. Effects of population growth in the Great Lakes region	○	○	○	○	○	○	○
c. Atmospheric deposition of pollutants from sources outside the Great Lakes basin	○	○	○	○	○	○	○
d. Inadequate infrastructure for wastewater or stormwater	○	○	○	○	○	○	○
e. Effects of natural events, such as drought	○	○	○	○	○	○	○
f. Removal of water from the Great Lakes for use outside of the region	○	○	○	○	○	○	○
g. Different policies among Great Lakes states	○	○	○	○	○	○	○
h. Insufficient coordination between the United States and Canada	○	○	○	○	○	○	○
i. Different priorities among restoration stakeholders	○	○	○	○	○	○	○
j. Other	○	○	○	○	○	○	○

For item i - Please specify which stakeholders you have found to have different priorities:	
For item j - Please specify the other factor(s) that may limit the restoration of the Great Lakes ecosystem:	

13. Looking at the above list of factors outside of the scope of the GLRI Action Plan that have the potential to affect the broader goal of restoring the health of the Great Lakes ecosystem, which would you say are the top three in terms of having the greatest potential to limit the restoration of the health of the Great Lakes ecosystem?

*(Enter the **letter designations (a-j)** from question 12 above.)*

The first most limiting factor is: ▭

The second most limiting factor is: ▭

10 of 12

The third most limiting factor is:

11 of 12

Section 8 - Improvements to the GLRI Program and Survey Completion Question

14. What suggestion or suggestions would you make to improve the GLRI?

15. Please provide any additional comments you may have about the GLRI or Great Lakes restoration in general.

16. Are you ready to submit your final completed survey to GAO?

(This is equivalent to mailing a completed paper survey to us. It tells us that your answers are official and final.)

○ Yes, my survey is complete - *To submit your final responses, please click on "Exit" below.*

◉ No, my survey is not yet complete - *To save your responses for later, please click on "Exit" below.*

You may view and print your completed survey by clicking on the Summary link in the menu to the left.

Thank you very much for your assistance.

| Print |
| Exit |

12 of 12

Appendix VI: Great Lakes Restoration Initiative Action Plan Long-term Goals, Objectives, and Measures of Progress for Each of the Five Focus Areas

The GLRI Action Plan for fiscal years 2010 to 2014 is organized by five focus areas that, according to the federal agencies responsible for implementing the GLRI, encompass the most significant environmental problems in the Great Lakes: (1) toxic substances and areas of concern; (2) invasive species; (3) nearshore health and nonpoint source pollution; (4) habitat and wildlife protection and restoration; and (5) accountability, education, monitoring, evaluation, communication and partnerships. Each focus area includes several long-term goals to address these problems, as well as objectives to be completed within the 5 years of the plan and measures of progress to ensure that efforts are on track to meet the long-term goals.

Focus Area One, Toxic Substances and Areas of Concern

Long-term Goals	
	• Goal 1: Areas of concern are cleaned up, restoring the areas and removing the beneficial use impairments.
	• Goal 2: The release of toxic substances in toxic amounts is prevented and the release of any or all persistent toxic substances to the Great Lakes Basin ecosystem is virtually eliminated.
	• Goal 3: Exposure to toxic substances from historically contaminated sources is significantly reduced through source reduction and other exposure reduction methods.
	• Goal 4: Environmental levels of toxic chemicals are reduced to the point that all restrictions on the consumption of Great Lakes fish can be lifted.
	• Goal 5: The health and integrity of wildlife populations and habitat are protected from adverse chemical and biological effects associated with the presence of toxic substances in the Great Lake Basin.

Objectives

- By 2014, delist five areas of concern.

- By 2014, 46 beneficial use impairments will be removed in areas of concern.

Appendix IV Great Lakes Restoration Initiative
Action Plan Long-term Goals, Objectives, and
Measures of Progress for Each of the Five
Focus Areas

- By 2011, 15 million pounds of electronic waste and 15 million pills of unwanted medicines will be collected or their release will have been prevented.

- By 2014, 45 million pounds of e-waste, 45 million pills of unwanted medicines, and 4.5 million pounds of household hazardous waste in the Great Lakes Basin will have been collected or their release will have been prevented.

- By 2014, 9.4 million cubic yards of contaminated sediments will be remediated.

- Through 2014, an annual average of up to 5 percent annual decline will be maintained or improved for the trend (year 2000 and on) in average concentrations of PCBs in whole lake trout and walleye samples.

Measures of Progress

- Number of areas of concern in the Great Lakes where all management actions necessary for delisting have been implemented (cumulative).

- Area of concern beneficial use impairments removed (cumulative).[1]

- Beneficial use impairment delisting project starts at areas of concern (cumulative).[2]

- Cubic yards (in millions) of contaminated sediment remediated in the Great Lakes (cumulative).[3]

- Pollution (in pounds) collected through prevention and waste minimization projects in the Great Lakes Basin (cumulative).

[1]This is an existing measure [used in the agency's performance plan and performance report, which are required by the Government Performance Results Act, as amended].

[2]These projects represent on-the-ground actions that are being implemented in order to remove beneficial use impairments. For example, sediment removals, Superfund cleanups, habitat projects and others.

[3]This is an existing measure [used in the agency's performance plan and performance report, which are required by the Government Performance Results Act, as amended].

Appendix II Great Lakes Restoration Initiative
Action Plan Long-term Goals, Objectives, and
Measures of Progress for Each of the Five
Focus Areas

- Cumulative percentage decline for the long term trend in average concentrations of PCBs in Great Lakes fish.[4]

Focus Area Two, Invasive Species

Long-term Goals	• Goal 1: The introduction of new invasive species to the Great Lakes Basin ecosystem is eliminated, reflecting a "zero tolerance policy" toward invasives.
	• Goal 2: The risk of introduction of species, which are imported for various uses, in the Great Lakes is minimized.
	• Goal 3: The spread of invasive species, by means of recreational activities, connecting waterways, and other vectors, beyond their current range is prevented.
	• Goal 4: A comprehensive program for detection and tracking newly identified invasive species in the Great Lakes is developed and provides up-to-date critical information needed by decision makers for evaluating potential rapid response actions.
	• Goal 5: An effective, efficient and environmentally sound program of integrated pest management for invasive species is developed and implemented, including program functions of containment, eradication, control, and mitigation.
Objectives	• By 2011, eight state aquatic nuisance species management plans will be established or revised to include rapid response capabilities. By 2014, eight state-based, multiagency rapid response plans will be implemented and 22 mock exercises to practice responses carried out under those plans and/or actual response actions will be completed.

---

[4]The annual decline is 5 percent per year. This is based on an existing measure [used in the agency's performance plan and performance report, which are required by the Government Performance Results Act, as amended]. In fiscal year 2010, 2008 data are compared to 2000 data; in fiscal year 2011, 2009 data are compared to 2000 data; and so forth. PCBs are one indicator for a broader suite of persistent toxic substances and one of a number being tracked.

Appendix II Great Lakes Restoration Initiative
Action Plan Long-term Goals, Objectives, and
Measures of Progress for Each of the Five
Focus Areas

- Six technologies that prevent the introduction of invasive species and four technologies that either contain or control invasive species will be developed or refined and piloted by 2011. Ten technologies that prevent the introduction of invasive species and five technologies that either contain or control invasive species will be developed or refined and piloted by 2014.

- By 2011, methodology and protocols will be piloted for the coordinated monitoring methodology and shared protocols for basinwide invasive species surveillance. By 2014, a basinwide surveillance program with shared sampling protocols and methodologies to provide early detection of nonnative species will be operational.

- By 2014, a 40 percent reduction in the yearly average rate of invasive species newly detected in the Great Lakes ecosystem will be achieved, compared with the period 2000-2009.

- By 2014, invasive species populations within the Great Lakes ecosystem will have been controlled and reduced, as measured in populations controlled to a target level in 6,500 acres of managed area and by removing 5,000 pounds of invasive species from the Great Lakes ecosystem.

- By 2014, approximately 10 million recreation and resource users will be educated on best practices that prevent the introduction and spread of invasive species.

Measures of Progress	

- Rate of nonnative species newly detected in the Great Lakes ecosystem.

- Acres managed for populations of invasive species controlled to a target level (cumulative).

- Number multiagency plans established, mock exercises to practice rapid responses carried out under those plans, and/or actual rapid response actions (cumulative).

- Number of recreation and resource users contacted on best practices that prevent the introduction and spread of invasive species (cumulative).

A□□en□i□ □l□Great Lakes Restoration Initiative
A□tion P□an Long-ter□ Goa□s□O□□e□tives□an□
□eas□res o□Progress □or □a□□ o□t□e □ive
□o□□s Areas

Focus Area Three, Nearshore Health and Nonpoint Source Pollution

Long-term Goals	
	• Goal 1: Nearshore aquatic communities consist of healthy, self-sustaining plant and animal populations dominated by native and naturalized species.
	• Goal 2: Land use, recreation, and economic activities are managed to ensure that nearshore aquatic, wetland, and upland habitats will sustain the health and function of natural communities.
	• Goal 3: The presence of bacteria, viruses, pathogens, nuisance growths of plants or animals, objectionable taste or odors, or other risks to human health are reduced to levels in which water quality standards are met and beneficial uses attained to protect human use and enjoyment of the nearshore areas.
	• Goal 4: High-quality bathing beach opportunities are maintained by eliminating impairments from bacterial, algal, and chemical contamination; effective monitoring for pathogens; effective modeling of environmental conditions, where appropriate; and timely communications to the public about beach health and daily swimming conditions.
	• Goal 5: A significant reduction in soil erosion and the loading of sediments, nutrients, and pollutants into tributaries is achieved through greater implementation of practices that conserve soil and slow overland flow in agriculture, forestry and urban areas.
	• Goal 6: High quality, timely and relevant information about the nearshore areas is readily available to assess progress and to inform enlightened decision making.
Objectives	• By 2010, EPA will compile and map the highest priority watersheds for implementation of targeted nonpoint source pollution control measures.

Appendix I Great Lakes Restoration Initiative
Action Plan Long-term Goals Objectives and
Measures of Progress for Each of the Five
Focus Areas

- By 2014, remediation, restoration and conservation actions in at least one targeted watershed in each Great Lake Basin will control erosion, reduce nutrient runoff from urban and agricultural sources, and improve habitat to protect nearshore aquatic resources.

- By 2014, a baseline will be established for total suspended solids loadings from targeted tributaries.

- By 2014, a measurable decrease will be achieved in soluble phosphorous loading from 2008 levels in targeted tributaries.

- By 2014, the causes of nutrient-related nearshore biological impairments will be better understood and, following local or watershed remedial actions, the number and severity of incidences of harmful algal blooms, avian botulism, and/or excessive *Cladophora* growth will be significantly reduced from 2008 levels.

- By 2014, a comprehensive nearshore monitoring program will have been established and implemented, including a publicly accessible reporting system, based on a suite of environmental indicators.

- By 2014, 50 percent of high-priority Great Lakes beaches will have been assessed using a standardized sanitary survey tool to identify sources of contamination.[5]

- By 2014, 20 percent of high-priority Great Lakes beaches will have begun to implement measures to control, manage or remediate pollution sources identified through the use of sanitary surveys.

- By 2014, rapid testing or predictive modeling methods (to improve the accuracy of decisions on beach postings to better protect public health) will be employed at 33 percent of high-priority beaches.
- By 2014, the area of agricultural lands in conservation and/or utilizing conservation tillage practices will increase by 50 percent over 2008 levels.

---

[5]Beaches that the states identify as most frequently used and/or that have the highest risk. In 2008, there were 356 high-priority beaches out a total of 1,411 total beaches in the U.S. Great Lakes.

Appendix I Great Lakes Restoration Initiative
Action Plan Long-term Goals Objectives and
Measures of Progress for Each of the Five
Focus Areas

Measures of Progress	
	• Five-year average annual loadings of soluble reactive phosphorous from tributaries draining targeted watersheds.[6]
	• Percentage of beaches meeting bacteria standards 95 percent or more of beach days.
	• Extent (sq. miles) of Great Lakes harmful algal blooms.[7]
	• Annual number of days U.S. Great Lakes beaches are closed or posted due to nuisance algae.[8]
	• Annual volume of sediment deposition in defined harbor areas in targeted watersheds (cubic yards).[9]
	• Acres in Great Lakes watershed with U.S. Department of Agriculture conservation practices implemented to reduce erosion, nutrients and/or pesticide loading under Farm Bill programs.[10]

[6][Measured in] metric tons per year. Total phosphorus will also be measured. Targeted watersheds will receive focused efforts toward restoration activities, for example, agricultural best management practices.

[7]Biological responses to nutrients loadings are also dependent on other factors such as water temperature, timing and intensity of precipitation, and hydrologic features. Year-to-year variability in these features may mask local improvements in nutrients management. Satellite imagery may provide data for days during which harmful algal blooms are reported by shoreline observers or boaters.

[8]This metric will be added to national surveys for beach managers for 2010. Nuisance algae can include *Cladophora*, harmful algal blooms or other species, all of which are believed to be aggravated by elevated levels of phosphorous in the water.

[9]U.S. Army Corps of Engineers dredges the federal shipping channel at Toledo Harbor each year. This area receives the highest rate of sedimentation in the Great Lakes, coming from the Maumee River watershed. Even small improvements in the rate of sedimentation here would reflect considerable efforts in the watershed to reduce erosion and farm runoff. Alternately, the Corps conducts bathymetric surveys of commercial harbors each year, from which the volume of new fluvial sediment can be calculated for targeted watersheds. Because the Corps does not dredge every location of every harbor each year, the estimated accumulation from a designated area over time will reflect the relative amount of sediments deposited from the tributary. This approach is currently in development.

[10]This measure reflects annual (not cumulative) implementation of conservation practices (from the Environmental Quality Incentives Program and Conservation Technical Assistance program) that will continue to contribute to long term improvements of the listed outcomes.

Appendix III Great Lakes Restoration Initiative
Action Plan Long-term Goals Objectives and
Measures of Progress for each of the Five
Focus Areas

Focus Area Four, Habitat and Wildlife Protection and Restoration

Long-term Goals	• Goal 1: Protection and restoration of Great Lakes aquatic and terrestrial habitats, including physical, chemical, and biological processes and ecosystem functions, maintain or improve the conditions of native fish and wildlife.
	• Goal 2: Critical management activities (such as stocking native fish and other aquatic species, restoring access of migratory fish species at fish passage barriers, and identifying and addressing diseases) protect and conserve important fish and wildlife populations.
	• Goal 3: Sound decision making is facilitated by accessible, site specific and landscape-scale baseline status and trend information about fish and wildlife resources and their habitats.
	• Goal 4: High-priority actions identified in strategic plans (such as state and federal species management, restoration and recovery plans, Lakewide Management Plans, Remedial Action Plans, and others) are implemented, lead to the achievement of plan goals, and reduce the loss of fish and wildlife and their habitats.
	• Goal 5: Development activities are planned and implemented in ways that are sensitive to environmental considerations and compatible with fish and wildlife and their habitats.
Objectives	• By 2014, 4,500 miles of Great Lakes rivers and tributaries will be reopened and 450 barriers to fish passage will be removed or bypassed.
	• By 2014, 82 percent of recovery actions for federally listed priority species will be implemented.
	• By 2014, 53 percent of populations of native aquatic non-threatened and endangered species are self-sustaining.
	• By 2014, 97,500 acres of wetlands, wetland-associated uplands, and high-priority coastal, upland, urban, and island habitats will be

Appendix I: Great Lakes Restoration Initiative
Action Plan Long-term Goals, Objectives, and
Measures of Progress for Each of the Five
Focus Areas

protected, restored or enhanced.

- By 2014, 100 percent of U.S. coastal wetlands in the Great Lakes Basin will be assessed.

- By 2014, 30 habitat-related beneficial use impairments will be delisted across the areas of concern.

Measures of Progress	

- Miles of rivers reopened for fish passage.

- Number of fish passage barriers removed or bypassed.

- Number of species delisted due to recovery.

- Percentage of recovery actions implemented for priority listed species.

- Percentage of populations of native aquatic non-threatened and endangered species self-sustaining in the wild.

- Number of acres of wetlands and wetland-associated uplands protected, restored and enhanced.

- Number of acres of coastal, upland, and island habitats protected, restored and enhanced.

- Percent of U.S. coastal Great Lakes wetlands assessed.

- Number of habitat-related beneficial use impairments removed from the 27 U.S. areas of concern so impaired.[11]

---

[11]Also captured under the second measure in focus area one.

Appendix II Great Lakes Restoration Initiative
Action Plan Long-term Goals, Objectives, and
Measures of Progress for Each of the Five
Focus Areas

Focus Area Five, Accountability, Education, Monitoring, Evaluation, Communication and Partnerships

Long-term Goals	• Goal 1: A cooperative monitoring and observing system provides a comprehensive assessment of the Great Lakes ecosystem.
	• Goal 2: The necessary technology and programmatic infrastructure supports monitoring and reporting, including Great Lakes Restoration Initiative project deliverables by all agencies and participating stakeholders. Data and information are provided in reports that are public friendly, timely and available on the Internet. Reports present integrated and scaled data from watersheds to lakes to Great Lakes basinwide.
	• Goal 3: Increase outreach and education for the Great Lakes, and provide ongoing K-12 education for students to understand the benefits and ecosystem functions of the Great Lakes so they are able to make decisions to ensure that restoration investments are enhanced over time.
	• Goal 4: Expand the range of opportunities for Great Lakes stakeholders and citizens to provide input to the governments and participate in Great Lakes issues and concerns.
	• Goal 5: Work under the goals and objectives of the Great Lakes Water Quality Agreement is coordinated between the United States and Canada through Lakewide Management Plans and other binational processes.
Objectives	• By 2011, opportunities for collaboration, planning, data accessibility and accountability will be increased through the expanded use of Internet-based technology.

Appendix III Great Lakes Restoration Initiative
Action Plan Long-term Goals, Objectives, and
Measures of Progress for Each of the Five
Focus Areas

- By 2011, an Accountability System will be developed and implemented for the Initiative. The system will integrate and make transparent strategic planning, budgeting, and results monitoring.

- By 2011, a satellite remote sensing program will be implemented to assess Great Lakes productivity and biological (e.g., algal bloom) events.

- By 2011, outreach and education efforts are increased, including identifying and revising existing curricula to incorporate sustainable education needs for the Great Lakes that meet state and other relevant learning standards.

- By 2011, a refined suite of science-based indicators for development of a comprehensive assessment of Great Lakes ecosystem health will be identified, monitoring programs for those indicators will begin to be implemented, and restoration and protection actions tied to those assessments and programs assured.

- By 2011, social media access opportunities for basinwide public involvement in the Initiative will be in place.

- By 2012, education efforts under existing curricula that meet state and other relevant learning standards will be coordinated across states, and a system for tracking student and teacher outreach (quantitatively and qualitatively) for their use.

- By 2012, improved coordination with Canada will take place for programs under the Great Lakes Water Quality Agreement, particularly under the Lakewide Management Plans, which will result in the achievement of 5-10 priority Lakewide Management Plans goals and actions.

- By 2014, a statistically valid and comprehensive assessment, using a probability-based design, of Great Lakes water resources, will be established. The system will integrate shipboard monitoring, remote sensing, automated sampling, and other monitoring or observing efforts. By 2016, the system will be in place for all of the Great Lakes and it will be capable of providing a scientifically justifiable assessment of Great Lakes water resources.

- By 2014, timely data and information will be provided to decision makers at multiple scales within a framework of established baselines, targets, indicators of progress, and monitoring.

Appendix I: Great Lakes Restoration Initiative
Action Plan Long-term Goals, Objectives, and
Measures of Progress for each of the Five
Focus Areas

Measures of Progress	• Improvement in the overall aquatic ecosystem health of the Great Lakes using the Great Lakes 40-point scale.[12] • Number of priority Lakewide Management Plans projects that are completed. • Number of educational institutions incorporating new or existing Great Lakes protection and stewardship criteria into their broader environment education curricula.[13]

---

[12]This is an existing measure [used in the agency's performance plan and performance report, which are required by the Government Performance Results Act, as amended]. The Great Lakes Index uses select Great Lakes ecosystem indicators (i.e., coastal wetlands, phosphorus concentrations, area of concern sediment contamination, benthic health, fish tissue contamination, beach closures, drinking water quality, and air toxics deposition) and is based on a 1 to 5 rating system for each indicator, where 1 is poor and 5 is good. Improvements in the index and measures would indicate that fewer toxics are entering the food chain; ecosystem and human health is better protected; fish are safer to eat; water is safer to drink; and beaches are safer for swimming.

[13]Educational institutions include: state departments of education, primary and secondary school districts, colleges, universities, zoos, aquaria, museums, and nature/resource centers. Curricula will meet relevant official standards.

Appendix VII: GAO Contact and Staff Acknowledgments

GAO Contact

J. Alfredo Gómez, (202) 512-3841 or gomezj@gao.gov

Staff Acknowledgments

In addition to the individual named above, Steven Elstein, Assistant Director; Krista Breen Anderson; Cheryl Arvidson; Mark Braza; Lisa L. Fisher; Stuart M. Kaufman; Armetha Liles; Marya Link; Michelle K. Treistman; and Wayne Turowski made significant contributions to this report.